LAYERS OF LEARNING

YEAR TWO • UNIT SEVEN

NORMANS
NIGERIA
SKELETONS
CANTERBURY TALES

Published by HooDoo Publishing
United States of America
ISBN 978-1495303982

UNITS AT A GLANCE: TOPICS FOR ALL FOUR YEARS OF THE LAYERS OF LEARNING PROGRAM

1	History	Geography	Science	The Arts
1	Mesopotamia	Maps & Globes	Planets	Cave Paintings
2	Egypt	Map Keys	Stars	Egyptian Art
3	Europe	Global Grids	Earth & Moon	Crafts
4	Ancient Greece	Wonders	Satellites	Greek Art
5	Babylon	Mapping People	Humans in Space	Poetry
6	The Levant	Physical Earth	Laws of Motion	List Poems
7	Phoenicians	Oceans	Motion	Moral Stories
8	Assyrians	Deserts	Fluids	Rhythm
9	Persians	Arctic	Waves	Melody
10	Ancient China	Forests	Machines	Chinese Art
11	Early Japan	Mountains	States of Matter	Line & Shape
12	Arabia	Rivers & Lakes	Atoms	Color & Value
13	Ancient India	Grasslands	Elements	Texture & Form
14	Ancient Africa	Africa	Bonding	African Tales
15	First North Americans	North America	Salts	Creative Kids
16	Ancient South America	South America	Plants	South American Art
17	Celts	Europe	Flowering Plants	Jewelry
18	Roman Republic	Asia	Trees	Roman Art
19	Christianity	Australia & Oceania	Simple Plants	Instruments
20	Roman Empire	You Explore	Fungi	Composing Music

2	History	Geography	Science	The Arts
1	Byzantines	Turkey	Climate & Seasons	Byzantine Art
2	Barbarians	Ireland	Forecasting	Illumination
3	Islam	Arabian Peninsula	Clouds & Precipitation	Creative Kids
4	Vikings	Norway	Special Effects	Viking Art
5	Anglo Saxons	Britain	Wild Weather	King Arthur Tales
6	Charlemagne	France	Cells and DNA	Carolingian Art
7	Normans	Nigeria	Skeletons	Canterbury Tales
8	Feudal System	Germany	Muscles, Skin, & Cardiopulmonary	Gothic Art
9	Crusades	Balkans	Digestive & Senses	Religious Art
10	Burgundy, Venice, Spain	Switzerland	Nerves	Oil Paints
11	Wars of the Roses	Russia	Health	Minstrels & Plays
12	Eastern Europe	Hungary	Metals	Printmaking
13	African Kingdoms	Mali	Carbon Chem	Textiles
14	Asian Kingdoms	Southeast Asia	Non-metals	Vivid Language
15	Mongols	Caucasus	Gases	Fun With Poetry
16	Medieval China & Japan	China	Electricity	Asian Arts
17	Pacific Peoples	Micronesia	Circuits	Arts of the Islands
18	American Peoples	Canada	Technology	Indian Legends
19	The Renaissance	Italy	Magnetism	Renaissance Art I
20	Explorers	Caribbean Sea	Motors	Renaissance Art II

3	History	Geography	Science	The Arts
1	Age of Exploration	Argentina and Chile	Classification & Insects	Fairy Tales
2	The Ottoman Empire	Egypt and Libya	Reptiles & Amphibians	Poetry
3	Mogul Empire	Pakistan & Afghanistan	Fish	Mogul Arts
4	Reformation	Angola & Zambia	Birds	Reformation Art
5	Renaissance England	Tanzania & Kenya	Mammals & Primates	Shakespeare
6	Thirty Years' War	Spain	Sound	Baroque Music
7	The Dutch	Netherlands	Light & Optics	Baroque Art I
8	France	Indonesia	Bending Light	Baroque Art II
9	The Enlightenment	Korean Pen.	Color	Art Journaling
10	Russia & Prussia	Central Asia	History of Science	Watercolors
11	Conquistadors	Baltic States	Igneous Rocks	Creative Kids
12	Settlers	Peru & Bolivia	Sedimentary Rocks	Native American Art
13	13 Colonies	Central America	Metamorphic Rocks	Settler Sayings
14	Slave Trade	Brazil	Gems & Minerals	Colonial Art
15	The South Pacific	Australasia	Fossils	Principles of Art
16	The British in India	India	Chemical Reactions	Classical Music
17	Boston Tea Party	Japan	Reversible Reactions	Folk Music
18	Founding Fathers	Iran	Compounds & Solutions	Rococo
19	Declaring Independence	Samoa and Tonga	Oxidation & Reduction	Creative Crafts I
20	The American Revolution	South Africa	Acids & Bases	Creative Crafts II

4	History	Geography	Science	The Arts
1	American Government	USA	Heat & Temperature	Patriotic Music
2	Expanding Nation	Pacific States	Motors & Engines	Tall Tales
3	Industrial Revolution	U.S. Landscapes	Energy	Romantic Art I
4	Revolutions	Mountain West States	Energy Sources	Romantic Art II
5	Africa	U.S. Political Maps	Energy Conversion	Impressionism I
6	The West	Southwest States	Earth Structure	Impressionism II
7	Civil War	National Parks	Plate Tectonics	Post-Impressionism
8	World War I	Plains States	Earthquakes	Expressionism
9	Totalitarianism	U.S. Economics	Volcanoes	Abstract Art
10	Great Depression	Heartland States	Mountain Building	Kinds of Art
11	World War II	Symbols and Landmarks	Chemistry of Air & Water	War Art
12	Modern East Asia	The South States	Food Chemistry	Modern Art
13	India's Independence	People of America	Industry	Pop Art
14	Israel	Appalachian States	Chemistry of Farming	Modern Music
15	Cold War	U.S. Territories	Chemistry of Medicine	Free Verse
16	Vietnam War	Atlantic States	Food Chains	Photography
17	Latin America	New England States	Animal Groups	Latin American Art
18	Civil Rights	Home State Study	Instincts	Theater & Film
19	Technology	Home State Study II	Habitats	Architecture
20	Terrorism	America in Review	Conservation	Creative Kids

www.layers-of-learning.com

Unit 2-7 Printable Pack

This unit includes printables at the end. To make life easier for you we also created digital printable packs for each unit. To retrieve your printable pack for Unit 2-7, please visit

www.layers-of-learning.com/digital-printable-packs/

Put the printable pack in your shopping cart and use this coupon code:

2007UNIT2-7

Your printable pack will be free.

LAYERS OF LEARNING INTRODUCTION

This is part of a series of units in the Layers of Learning homeschool curriculum, including the subjects of history, geography, science, and the arts. Children from 1st through 12th can participate in the same curriculum at the same time – family school style.

The units are intended to be used in order as the basis of a complete curriculum (once you add in a systematic math, reading, and writing program). You begin with Year 1 Unit 1 no matter what ages your children are. Spend about 2 weeks on each unit. You pick and choose the activities within the unit that appeal to you and read the books from the book list that are available to you or find others on the same topic from your library. We highly recommend that you use the timeline in every history section as the backbone. Then flesh out your learning with reading and activities that highlight the topics you think are the most important.

Alternatively, you can use the units as activity ideas to supplement another curriculum in any order you wish. You can still use them with all ages of children at the same time.

When you've finished with Year One, move on to Year Two, Year Three, and Year Four. Then begin again with Year One and work your way through the years again. Now your children will be older, reading more involved books, and writing more in depth. When you have completed the sequence for the second time, you start again on it for the third and final time. If your student began with Layers of Learning in 1st grade and stayed with it all the way through she would go through the four year rotation three times, firmly cementing the information in her mind in ever increasing depth. At each level you should expect increasing amounts of outside reading and writing. High schoolers in particular should be reading extensively, and if possible, participating in discussion groups.

☺ ☻ ☻ These icons will guide you in spotting activities and books that are appropriate for the age of child you are working with. But if you think an activity is too juvenile or too difficult for your kids, adjust accordingly. The icons are not there as rules, just guides.

☺ GRADES 1-4

☻ GRADES 5-8

☻ GRADES 9-12

Within each unit we share:
- EXPLORATIONS, activities relating to the topic;
- EXPERIMENTS, usually associated with science topics;
- EXPEDITIONS, field trips;
- EXPLANATIONS, teacher helps or educational philosophies.

In the sidebars we also include Additional Layers, Famous Folks, Fabulous Facts, On the Web, and other extra related topics that can take you off on tangents, exploring the world and your interests with a bit more freedom. The curriculum will always be there to pull you back on track when you're ready.

You can learn more about how to use this curriculum at www.layers-of-learning.com/layers-of-learning-program/

UNIT SEVEN
NORMANS – NIGERIA – SKELETONS – CANTERBURY TALES

Never force yourself to read a book that you do not enjoy. There are so many good books in the world that it is foolish to waste time on one that does not give you pleasure.
-Atwood H. Townsend

	LIBRARY LIST:
HISTORY	Search for: Normans, 1066, William the Conqueror, Empress Matilda, Thomas a Becket, Scottish Wars of Independence, William Wallace, Robert the Bruce, Hundred Years War, Joan of Arc

☺ 1066: The Crown, the Comet, and the Conqueror by David Hobbs.

☺ ☻ Joan of Arc by Dianne Stanley. A perfect read-aloud for younger kids

☺ ☻ Joan of Arc by Josephine Poole. Picture book.

☺ ☻ An Illustrated History of 1066 by Charles Jones.

☻ The King's Shadow by Elizabeth Alder. A young boy finds himself a servant of King Harold of England as Harold battles to save his kingdom from invasion. See other books in the series.

☻ The Red Keep: A Story of Burgundy in 1165 by Allen French. A robber baron is threatening the countryside.

☻ If All The Swords in England by Barbara Willard. Tells the story of King Henry II and Thomas a' Beckett.

☻ The Beggars Bible by Louis A. Vernon. Novel about John Wycliffe, who translated the Bible into English.

☺ ☻ Wulf the Saxon by G. A. Henty. A young Saxon boy joins Harold's army to fight against the invaders in 1066.

☺ ☻ The Heroes of Scotland DVD tells the story of Robert Roy, William Wallace, and Robert the Bruce.

☺ ☻ In Freedom's Cause by G.A. Henty. Tells the story of Wallace and Bruce.

☺ ☻ St. George for England by G.A. Henty. Story of the battles of Crecy and Poitier.

☺ ☻ Both Sides the Border by G.A. Henty. Story of the struggle to free Wales from English rule.

☺ ☻ At Agincourt by G.A. Henty. Tells the story of the battle of Agincourt plus the events that lead up to it and the aftermath through the device of a fictional hero.

☻ 1066: the Year of Conquest by David Howarth. A must read.

☻ William Wallace: Braveheart by James Mackay.

☻ Joan of Arc by Mark Twain. Not your typical tongue in cheek Twain adventure, but the true story of Joan of Arc. Twain believed this book to be his finest.

☻ The Hundred Years War by Robin Neillands. Short, but thorough.

☻ Cur Deus Homo by Anselm.

GEOGRAPHY	Search for: Nigeria ☺ ☻ ☻ <u>Off to the Sweet Shores of Africa</u> by Uzi Unobagha. A picture book for all ages told with the rhythms of the talking drum and in the cultures of Africa. ☺ ☻ ☻ <u>Why the Sky is Far Away</u> by Mary-Joan Gerson. A picture book of an old Nigerian Folk Tale. The message of the tale is to curb our greed and use our resources wisely. ☺ ☻ ☻ <u>A Is For Africa</u> by Ifeoma Onyefulu. Photos and customs of Nigeria specifically and West Africa generally. Look for more titles by this Nigerian author. ☺ <u>One Big Family</u> by Ifeoma Onyefulu. Spend a day in a Nigerian village and understand the customs and social structure. ☺ <u>Talking Drums of Africa</u> by Christine Price. Picture book of how the drums are made and used in West Africa. ☺ ☻ <u>Ikenna Goes to Nigeria</u> by Ifeoma Onyefulu. The reader gets to go along with a young boy as he returns to his roots and visits his family in Nigeria. ☻ <u>Nigeria A to Z</u> by Tamra Orr. An overview of the county of Nigeria.
SCIENCE	Search for: bones, skeleton, skeletal system, joints ☺ ☻ ☻ <u>Human Anatomy Coloring Book</u> by Margaret Matt and Joe Ziemian. From Dover publishers, it's inexpensive enough for each of the kids to have their own. Highly recommended for use throughout the human anatomy units. There's more than you possibly get to in one year. Save the book for the next time you go through this stuff. ☺ ☻ <u>Skeleton</u> by Steve Parker. From the publisher DK, this book is full of pictures and full color graphics plus tons of information in small snippets. Read aloud with your younger students or hand over to a middle schooler to pour over.
THE ARTS	Search for: Canterbury Tales, Chaucer ☺ <u>Chanticleer and the Fox</u> by Barbara Cooney. A Caldecott winner, this picture book is the nun's Priest's Tale from Chaucer. ☻ <u>Chaucer's Canterbury Tales</u> by Marcia Williams. Tells the tales in modern English with lots of illustrations in a comic book format. Also includes carefully chosen snippets in Middle English in conversation bubbles within the illustrations. True to Chaucer, it contains some rude humor. ☻ <u>The Canterbury Tales</u> by Geoffrey Chaucer, trans. Geraldine McCaughrean. This is a retelling of the tales for middle grades and up. It is told in a comfortable and light style, more like the original intent of the tales. Not all of the tales are included (leaving out the more bawdy ones) and there is no middle English included. ☻ <u>The Canterbury Tales: A Retelling</u> by Peter Ackroyd. For high school and up, almost completely modern language patterns and words, but true to the original story. The only problem is that this version is more expensive. Check the library. ☻ <u>The Canterbury Tales Selections</u> by Geoffrey Chaucer, trans. Colin Wilcockson. From Penguin publishers. If you want a more scholarly version for your high schooler, this is the one to get. Includes only the most commonly studied tales so as not to overburden the young scholar. This is a more literal translation, but still no middle English. We highly recommend the Cliff's Notes to go with this one if you aren't a high school English teacher.

HISTORY: NORMANS

Famous Folks

Harold Godwinson is one of the most tragic and noble figures of history. He was king of England upon the death of Edward the Confessor in the year 1066, duly appointed by the Wittengamot, but was killed during the Battle of Hastings in that same year.

Fabulous Fact

The Normans were Vikings who had begun to settle in northern France from about 880.

Additional Layer

The Normans were the first European armored and mounted knights. At first knights were nothing but professional soldiers, all seeking land, power, and wealth, which made them lawless bandits more often than not. Normans were almost continually at war.

The English king, Edward the Confessor, was a very pious man, but not a very good ruler. He had spent most of his youth across the channel in Normandy and felt closer ties to those people than to his own. Near the end of his life he made a verbal promise to William of Normandy that he would leave the throne of England to William. There was one problem. Edward didn't have the power to do that. The kings council elected the next king from among those of royal blood and William, as a foreigner, didn't stand a chance. The council elected Harold instead.

William disagreed with the choice. Ignoring the laws of England and the wishes of the English people who loved Harold, he prepared for battle. Unfortunately, King Harold of Norway also had his sights set on England and was preparing his own invasion force. Harold summoned the levy of troops and marched his men north to Stamford Bridge where he fought a tough battle, but defeated the Norwegians. Then he had to turn around and force march his men back south where William was busy landing on the beach at Hastings. A violent battle was fought at Hastings where the English were beaten soundly and Harold himself was killed. William claimed England by right of conquest and instituted feudalism and the hereditary divine right of kings, destroying the rights of the free Englishmen in the process. The English didn't just sit by and watch it happen. They resisted for years and William ruled a fractious land. It was ten generations before England was healed.

William invaded England by sea across the English channel, something no one has successfully repeated since.

This leads us into the Hundred Years' War, which was the beginning of the animosity between the French and the English which lasted up until World War I. The royal families of Europe had a habit of marrying one another, first for diplomatic reasons and also because no one but a prince or king was worthy to marry a princess or a queen in their view. The family lines became so entangled that the next in line for the throne could be a confusing issue. That is why you see German kings ruling England and English ones ruling France on occasion. Whenever there was a succession there was a scramble to see who could gain power; this often led to war. The first of these conflicts was the Hundred Years' War. It started in 1337 with an English King named Edward and ended in 1453 with a French peasant girl named Joan.

Joan of Arc at the moment when she is first called to save France by her angels. Painting by Jules Bastien-Lepage, 1875.

The period in this section covers about 400 years of English history. More events are included in the timeline than are discussed in detail. Use the timeline as a guide to learn more about some of the important stuff happening in England during this period. We will cover the Black Death, the Magna Charta, the Peasant Revolts, and the crusades in future units.

Additional Layer

In this painting by Hermann Stilke (1843) we see Joan of Arc being burned at the stake. She didn't have to die, she could have recanted and denied her visions, but though tempted, in the end she stood by her story. Talk about courage and things worth dying for.

Fabulous Fact
In 1337 the English king owed allegiance to the French king, since the English king was also the Duke of Normandy. Edward III refused to pay homage and had his French lands confiscated, thus we begin over a hundred years of war.

Fabulous Fact
Over the course of the wars France lost about half her population to illness, banditry, and civil war.

Famous Folks

Tostig, Earl of Northumbria, and brother to King Harold, was cruel and heavy handed in his rule of his earldom. He had to be punished and exiled by Harold early in his reign. Tostig fled to Harold Hardrada and helped him plan his invasion which resulted in the battle at Stamford Bridge.

Without Tostig's rebellion, William's invasion would never have succeeded.

Fabulous Fact

The Normans and the Saxons were both of the same Germanic stock, but their traditions and language had diverged in the hundreds of years of separation on either side of the English channel. The Saxons maintained their freedom and independence and their common law codes, but the Normans had adopted the top down legislative law codes of the Romans and Franks, a combination of Salic and Justinian Law.

The year 1066 was a massive step backward for freedom in the world, a step that began to be righted in the year 1215.

☺ ☺ ☻ EXPLORATION: Battle of Hastings

Color a map of Harold's gallant defense of England in 1066 and William's new lands. Use the Battle of Hastings map from the end of this unit.

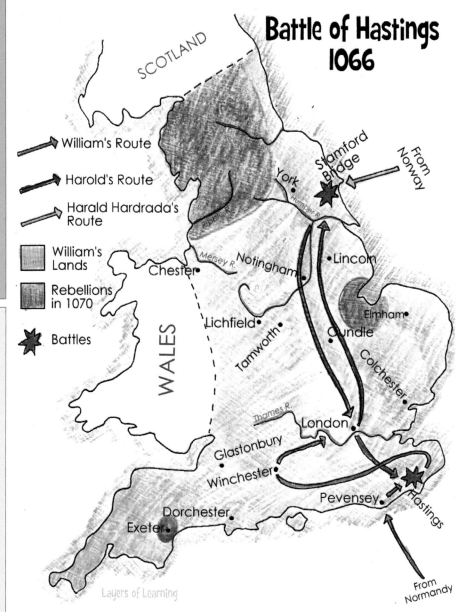

Harold had been watching the southern coast all summer, knowing William intended to invade. The time was nearly up for the fyrd and they would soon go home to their farms. Then he got word that Harald Hardrada had landed near York in the north. He rushed north with his men, picking up members of the fyrd as he traveled. He soundly defeated Harald at Stamford Bridge, but with great loss. Then immediately he turned around and force marched back to London, his men following as best they could. Meanwhile William had landed unopposed at Pevensey. Harold decided to march to meet him before his army was all gathered but also before William could march through the countryside bringing fire and death to his people. Harald himself led his weakened troops into battle and died there heroically defending his land.

☺ ☺ ☻ **EXPLORATION: Timeline**
You can find the printable timeline squares at the end of this unit.

- 1042-1066 Reign of Edward the Confessor; Harold elected as successor
- Sept 1066 Harald Hardrada of Norway is defeated at Stamford bridge
- October 1066 Battle of Hastings; William becomes king
- 1069-1070 English in the north rebel and William ruthlessly puts down the rebellion
- 1135 War of succession between Matilda and Stephen, lasts 19 years; period known as "The Anarchy"
- 1170 Thomas a Becket is killed in Canterbury Cathedral
- 1275 Parliament begins to meet regularly in England
- 1284 England annexes Wales and crown prince is known as Prince of Wales from then on
- 1290 Edward expels Jews from England, culminating hundreds of years of persecution; in 1182 they had been driven from France
- 1296 Edward deposes Scot king, John Balliol
- 1297 Battle of Cambuskenneth, Scot, William Wallace, defeats English
- 1298 Battle of Falkirk, English defeat William Wallace
- 1305 William Wallace captured and executed
- 1306 Robert the Bruce defeats English again in Scotland and is crowned king of Scots
- 1314 Battle of Bannockburn, Scots defeat English
- 1315-16 Famines in Europe mark a definite end to the prosperity of the High Middle Ages
- 1324-84 Life of religious reformer, John Wycliffe
- 1337 Start of 100 Years War
- 1340 Naval battle of Sluys, victory for England
- 1340 Geoffrey Chaucer born
- 1340 English Parliament declares exclusive right to tax
- 1346 Battle of Crecy, English victory
- 1356 Battle of Poitiers, English victory
- 1381 Peasants revolt and march on London
- 1415 Battle of Agincourt, English beat French
- 1429 Joan of Arc relieves the city of Orleans and helps

Famous Folks

Empress Matilda was the only and legal heir to the throne of England when her father, Henry I, died. Her throne was usurped by her cousin, Stephen, when she was pregnant in Normandy. She and Stephen fought over the throne for years resulting in bloody civil war. Though Matilda never regained the throne, she did assure that her son, Henry II, became king.

Additional Layer

Here is a student made video of the Hundred Years' War.

http://youtu.be/zxwTNvK6Gog

Make your own video depicting part of the Hundred Years War, the Scottish War for Independence, the events of 1066 or something else from this timeline.

Additional Layer

Thomas a Becket was the Archbishop of Canterbury from 1162 until 1170, when he was murdered in the cathedral on the orders of Henry II. Find out why Henry wanted him dead . . . or did he?

On the Web

Visit www.essentialnormanconquest.com. You will find interactive maps of the Battle of Hastings, information about what soldiers wore, an actual panoramic view of the battlefield as it is today, and more.

Additional Layer

Bayeux is a town in Normandy on the coast. It is where the tapestry was preserved and displayed for hundreds of years, though scholars now think it was actually made in England.

Charles VII to be crowned king at Rheims
- 1430 Burgundians capture Joan of Arc and give her to the English; she is burned the next year
- 1453 100 Years war ends, English lose all continental territories

☺ ☺ ☻ EXPLORATION: The Bayeux Tapestry

The Bayeux Tapestry is a piece of cloth that is 230 feet long! It is like a timeline, showing all kinds of famous events that lead up to the Norman conquest of England. The fabric tells us all kinds of stories from the time, from wars that were fought, kings crowned, and scandals revealed. It seems that some pieces are missing from it, so it may originally have been even longer. This is just one small scene of many from the the piece of cloth:

The Bayeux Tapestry is actually not a tapestry at all, but an embroidery. A tapestry has the pictures woven directly into the cloth. An embroidery is a piece of woven cloth with a picture stitched on to it. Embroidery is pretty simple, though the Bayeux tapestry, with its 50 plus detailed scenes would have been anything but simple to make! Still, you can create your own simple embroidery to try it out. You'll need a needle, 2 small pieces of cloth, a small piece of quilt batting, scissors, and some embroidery floss. All of these can be found at any craft store.

First, you layer a piece of fabric, a thin piece of quilt batting, and then a second piece of fabric on top of each other. Cut out a simple design using all 3 layers. Thread several strands of embroidery floss on to your needle, and tie a knot at the end using ends of the strands.

Next, begin on the back side of your design and poke your needle up through the layers of fabric, pulling the thread tight. Then go back down into the next spot. You can make tiny stitches all the way around your design or take large stitches as pictured below (these work well for younger children).

Continue stitching until you've completed your design. When you're done, you'll just tie off the threads using a small knot on the back of the design, then trim the thread off.

You can look online for lots of really detailed embroidery designs and tutorials if you want to do a more advanced version of this project.

☺ ☻ ☻ EXPLORATION: English Civil Wars

The English have had many civil wars, wars of succession and the like. During war it is always the weakest who suffer most. After having sworn fealty to Matilda as the next monarch of England, the nobles, not wanting to have a woman rule over them, accepted the weak King Stephan as king in her stead. Matilda fought for her throne through years of civil war. Under Stephen the land became overrun with robber barons and lawlessness, because Stephen was too nice to make his earls and nobles keep the peace. Here is what the Anglo-Saxon Chronicle says of this time:

In the days of this King there was nothing but strife, evil and robbery, for quickly the great men who were traitors rose against him. When the traitors saw that Stephen was a mild

Additional Layer

The period of civil war between Matilda and Stephen is called "the Anarchy", a fitting name and a fine example of what anarchy really brings.

Why do you think we need government?

Fabulous Fact

In 1140 England's lands stood thus: red, in Stephan's control; blue, in Matilda's control; gray native Welsh lands.

Additional Layer

The *Cadfael* mystery novels of Ellis Peters take place in the market town of Shrewsbury, near the Welsh border during the wars between Matilda and Stephen. Cadfael is a Benedictine monk at an abbey which is still standing.

Shrewsbury Abbey

good humoured man who inflicted no punishment, then they committed all manner of horrible crimes. They had done him homage and sworn oaths of fealty to him, but not one of their oaths was kept. They were all forsworn and their oaths broken. For every great man built him castles and held them against the king; they sorely burdened the unhappy people of the country with forced labour on the castles; and when the castles were built they filled them with devils and wicked men. By night and by day they seized those they believed to have any wealth, whether they were men or women; and in order to get their gold or silver, they put them into prison and tortured them with unspeakable tortures, for never were martyrs tortured as they were. They hung them up by the feet and smoked them with foul smoke. They strung them up by the thumbs, or by the head, and hung coats of mail on their feet. They tied knotted cords round their heads and twisted it until it entered the brain. They put them in dungeons wherein were adders and snakes and toads and so destroyed them. Many thousands they starved to death. I know not how to, nor am I able to tell of, all the atrocities nor all the cruelties which they wrought upon the unhappy people of this country. It lasted throughout the nineteen years that Stephen was king, and always grew worse and worse. Never did a country endure greater misery, and never did the heathen act more vilely than they did.

And so it lasted for nineteen long years while Stephen was King, till the land was all undone and darkened with such deeds and men said openly that Christ and his saints slept.

A weak or corrupt government allows evil to thrive and the people to suffer. Good government keeps evil at bay and allows ordinary people to live their lives in peace.

Make two paper castles to represent the power of the government. Print the castle craft from the end of this unit. Then color one castle to represent evil government and one to represent good government. Write traits of government on slips of paper and have the kids decide which castle each strip should go into. Some word strips are provided with the castle printable.

☺ ☻ EXPLORATION: Edward III's Coat of Arms

Edward III's coat of arms was changed from the lions of England to a combination of the lions quartered with the French fleur de lis. The lion was first used as the symbol of the English monarch by Henry II, then changed to the three lions by Richard I. The French fleur de lis was first used by Louis VI as his royal symbol. Fleur de lis means flower of the lily and the symbol is a stylized lily which represents perfection, light, and life. Edward chose to change his coat of arms when he claimed the throne of France.

Color the picture of the coat of arms from the end of this unit. The background of the fleur de lis is royal blue and the fleur de lis are yellow. The lions are yellow with a red background. You can cut it out and glue it to your own cardboard shield if you'd like.

☺ ☻ ☻ EXPLORATION: Scottish War of Independence

The Scottish War of Independence was fought for freedom from the English, who were forever trying to conquer their neighbors. A hero who emerged from this time is the Scotsman William Wallace, also known as Braveheart.

Wallace's most famous battle was at Stirling Bridge. The nobles of Scotland had already sold out to the English, so Wallace's army was made up almost entirely of Scottish peasants on foot with spears and axes for weapons. Wallace had taken up a position in the hills to the north of Stirling Bridge where he could watch the

English as they assembled and deployed their troops. The English were the foremost fighting force in Europe at that time and their heavy cavalry was unbeatable. But Wallace had chosen his ground well. The Stirling Bridge was barely wide enough for two horses to cross abreast, and after the bridge was a long causeway of the same width through a marsh. Though foot soldiers could navigate through the marsh, a horse weighted down with an armored knight would flounder and sink into the muck.

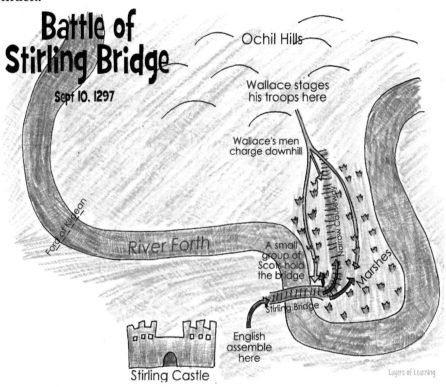

The English had the option of using the Ford of Kildean, where they could have crossed many more men over and flanked the Scots on dry ground, but they chose not to because of arrogance at their own fighting ability and a mistrust of the Scottish Laird, a traitor who had joined their cause and had suggested the ford.

The English crossed the bridge, and when about a third of the troops were across and before the cavalry had reached open ground, Wallace charged his men down the hill and into the English ranks who were bottled up and mired down. A small group of Scots fought their way to the head of the bridge and held back more English from crossing. The English who had crossed already were pushed back toward the river, many of them trampled under the hooves of their own horses as they made a mad scramble for the safety of the narrow bridge. Many soldiers and knights were drowned in the river as their heavy armor dragged them down. A few escaped by stripping their armor off and swimming the river. The English who crossed the bridge were almost killed to a man. The Scots however, suffered only light losses. It was a phenomenal victory, for it showed that not only could the English knights be defeated, but they could be defeated on foot with peasant soldiers. The news of their victory bolstered the French who were also at war with England.

Re-enact the battle. Set up your battle field in your yard or your living room. Represent the hills, the river, the bridge, the marsh, and the castle with objects or signs. Have three English soldiers for every one Scot. You can use stuffed animals to fill out the troops. Then have the troops act out the battle. There is also a printable of the battle at the end of this unit to color.

😐 😊 😃 **EXPLORATION: Hundred Years War Map**
Color a map of the Hundred Years War. Use the Hundred Years War map from the end of this unit. Color English, French, and Burgundian land from the early war years until the late years of the war. At the beginning of the war the English held some French land and the English king was a vassal of the French king. England gained vast territory in France during the war. But by the end of the war France took back control of all the English and most Burgundian lands thanks to Joan of Arc. After that, France's borders were similar to what they are today and the English no longer had any possessions on the continent, except the town of Calais.

Additional Layer

Scotland won both of their wars against the English. So why are they part of the United Kingdom today?

In 1707 Scotland and England signed a *Treaty of Union*. The two countries had been ruled by the same monarch since James VI, already king of Scotland, inherited the English crown from his distant cousin Elizabeth I in 1603.

Additional Layer

Learn more about the events of the two Scottish wars of independence and make a detailed timeline.

Writer's Workshop

Write a report on one of the books you read for this unit.

Famous Folks

Edward I, nicknamed Longshanks for his long legs, was called in to arbitrate between several claimants to the Scottish throne, but decided he'd quite like the throne for himself, thereby starting a series of bloody wars which would be carried on by his son and grandson.

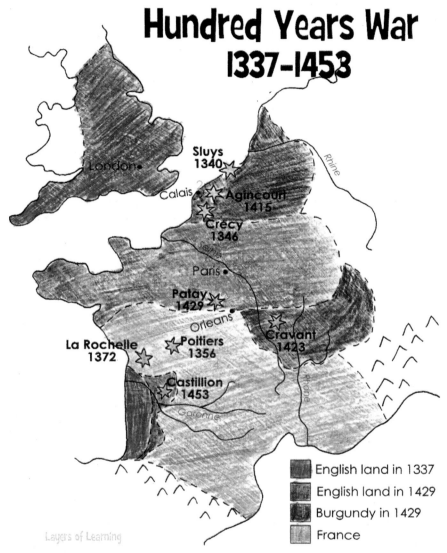

Hundred Years War
1337-1453

English land in 1337
English land in 1429
Burgundy in 1429
France

☺ ☻ **EXPLORATION: The Hundred Years' War**

The Hundred Years' War was a series of many battles between France and England over French lands. There was a lot of dispute over who should own those lands, mostly because so many royals of both families had intermarried so much that they both felt ties and ownership over it.

The English had a weapons advantage over the French. They used both cannons and longbows. Longbows were pretty inexpensive to make, but they could be used to shoot arrows about the length of 2 football fields. The arrows could take down the horses and penetrate the armor of the knights of France, who were fighting mostly with swords. The cannons were more frightening than anything, but to the French, these weapons seemed difficult to defeat. The French, however, were fighting for their own lands, and so fought bravely. They also had Joan of Arc on their side.

The English had taken over most of France until Joan started leading the French forces. She turned the war around, and even after her death France continued to win. They eventually drove the English forces out and regained power over their own country.

Make a lapbook of the Hundred Years' War. Start with a blank file folder. On the cover, write "Hundred Years' War" and decorate it if you like. Inside the folder add flaps of paper that can be lifted to reveal facts about the Hundred Years' War. Your student will have to do research to fill up their lap book. Include facts and images about famous people, important battles, weaponry, technology, maps, graphs of deaths, family trees of kings, a timeline, and anything else you come across in your reading.

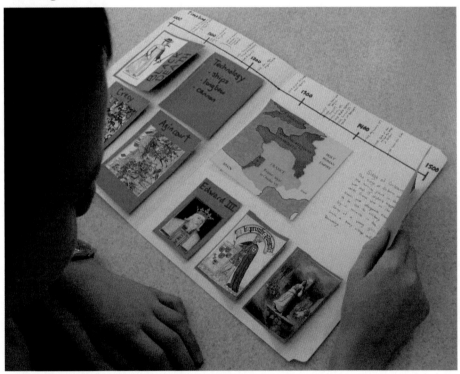

☺ ☻ ☻ EXPLORATION: Joan of Arc

Joan of Arc was just a French peasant girl, seventeen years old, who could neither read nor write. She had no power or influence, but she was determined to make a difference for her people. She believed it was her destiny to lead her people.

She went to see King Charles II. He had heard of her, and decided to test the young girl. He dressed in soldier's clothes and walked among his men while one of his advisers was dressed in his royal robes. The king wanted to see if she would know him even when disguised. When Joan of Arc came she barely even

Additional Layer

This period is the height of chivalry, or the code of honor for mounted soldiers. They committed to personal standards in training and prowess and also made vows to protect the weak including women and children and to defend the church. Knights were to never show cowardice and they were never to refuse a challenge from a foe.

Additional Layer

Remember how we mentioned that English kings saw England as a province of France? Well the French also saw France as a province of France, that is they were loyal to their local lords, but not to the king of France. The Hundred Years War changed that. The French began to take pride in France and thought of it as one country. Joan had a great deal to do with that. The English also began to think of England as a country worth being proud of and the old line between Normans and Saxons slowly began to disappear into Englishmen.

But France and England, they still really don't get along.

acknowledged the man on the throne, but instead walked right up to the disguised king. Impressed, he gave her command of an army of more than 12,000 men.

She won battle after battle. She became a true leader and was a brilliant strategist. She fought even when injured and was respected by all. Eventually she was captured and burned at the stake by the English. King Charles never even tried to rescue her.

Joan seemed very different than other young girls during her time. She was mocked, laughed at, and scorned. Even once she was the commander of all those troops people laughed at her. It took her a long time to really gain respect as a leader. Eventually her determination, insight, courage, and integrity gained her the respect of the people.

Have a discussion about how being different from others can be difficult, especially when we are laughed at. What qualities did Joan possess that earned her respect? Was her death proof that she shouldn't have tried to stand up for her people? Was she a hero? What makes someone a hero?

☺ ☻ EXPLORATION: Cannons
Cannons were used for the first time in Europe during the Hundred Years War. They gave the English soldiers a distinct advantage at the beginning of the war. The Chinese and Arabs had used cannons for centuries prior.

Make a model medieval cannon. You need clay, Popsicle sticks, and toothpicks for this project. Make a vase shaped body out of clay for the cannon, about 2 inches long.

Then set the cannon on a frame made of Popsicle sticks.

The cannon would lie on a wagon bed or, if fixed, on the walls of a city or castle to be fired. The cannoner would light the charge with a long red-hot iron. The charge was stuffed down inside and then iron bolts, like arrows, were stuffed in with the pointed ends protruding. When the cannon fired, the bolts would shoot toward the massed enemy troops and hopefully wreak some havoc. Sometimes small iron balls, like shot, would be stuffed in the cannon. The

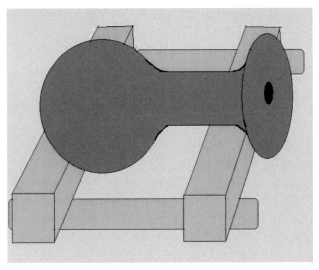

forging of large iron balls was not possible yet at this stage.

Use the toothpicks to represent the bolts.

Later cannons were mounted on wheels so they could be moved around a battlefield.

☺ ☻ ☻ EXPLORATION: Thanks Mailman

In the days of the Hundred Years War there was no simple way to communicate long distances. You couldn't just pick up a phone or zip an e-mail to your friend. The lords who were off fighting

the war used soot as ink and wrote on pieces of parchment. Then they tied the parchment in a scroll with a string, then sealed it with a wax seal, pressing their mark into the seal.

Imagine that you are a lord writing back to your subjects on your manor about the Hundred Years War. Tell what you've seen, roll up your letter, and tie it with a string. If you'd like to, you can drop some hot wax on to it and press a rubber stamp in to represent your seal. Now you just have to find someone traveling that way and send your letter off!

☺ ☻ ☻ EXPLORATION: Overview of the 100 Years War

If you don't have any great books to read about this war, you can use this website as a resource:
http://www.theotherside.co.uk/tm-heritage/background/100yearswar.htm

Additional Layer

The English besieged the town of Calais in 1347 for eleven months before the six leading burghers of the town offered their lives as forfeit if the rest of the townsfolk could leave the town in peace. King Edward III's wife begged that the lives of the six leaders would also be spared and they were. The town remained an English port until 1558.

Famous Folks

Medieval scientist and Franciscan friar Roger Bacon was the first Englishman to describe the composition of gunpowder in 1216.

Statue of Roger Bacon, photo by Michael Reeve and shared under CC license.

Fabulous Fact

By the end of the Hundred Years War cannons would begin to become significant forces in warfare.

On the Web

Check out this neat interactive map about the Hundred Years War by National Geographic. http://www.glencoe.com/sites/common_assets/socialstudies/in_motion_08/jat/p_367.swf

You may want to return to it several times throughout the unit as you learn about various battles and events.

Explanation

We have a little section of our bookshelf set aside for books we've made ourselves. I usually have them spiral bound at our local copy center. We usually leave a blank page at the back that is reserved for comments. When someone reads the book they can write a little comment saying what they like about it or congratulating the author on a job well done. The kids love to read the books they've written themselves, and it makes for a constant great review of things we've learned.

Karen

Designate each section of the website as a page. Write the topic at the top of the page, read the passage, and then write about it in your own words. Illustrate the section before moving on to the next section. By the end you'll have a basic storybook of the events of the Hundred Years War. Design a cover and bind the book so you'll have your own homemade reference book.

☺ ☻ EXPLORATION: John Wycliffe

John Wycliffe was an English theologian and professor at Oxford University during the 14th century. He believed the Church should have no influence over politics and neither should it administer properties and act as landlord. He also believed that the Bible should be translated into the common language of the people. He and his associates did in fact translate the Bible into English from the Latin Vulgate in 1384. His ideas were radical for his time. The Protestant Reformation wouldn't take place for well over one hundred years. For this reason he is sometimes called "the Morning Star of the Reformation".

Wycliffe was not content to keep his arguments within the walls of Oxford, but wrote extensive and plentiful tracts that were widely read throughout England. He also organized a troupe of poor preachers to travel through England preaching his simple version of the Gospel. He had the support of the English ruler, John of Gaunt, but not the church, which had a great deal of influence and wealth to lose if people agreed with Wycliffe. He did indeed gain a great following among the nobility, among scholars, and most dangerous of all, among the common people. His followers were known as Lollards.

After his natural death he was declared a heretic, his body exhumed and burned. His followers, led by Jan Hus, were persecuted, Hus was burned at the stake and a series of wars in central Europe followed. Wycliffe's greatest crime was in trying to destroy the secular power of the church. None of the conflicts were really over doctrine; they were over power, just as the later Reformation movement would be.

Read this biography in story form to your kids: http://www.wholesomewords.org/children/biocc/biowycliffecc.html

Then have them draw a scene of John Wycliffe or his followers from the story. Under the picture have them write this quote from Wycliffe: *I believe that in the end the truth will conquer.*

Do you believe that truth usually wins eventually?

GEOGRAPHY: NIGERIA

Nigeria is in west Africa. The southern edge of the country is on the Gulf of Guinea. In the south there are tropical rain forests. As you move northward the land gets progressively drier, moving through savanna until you reach the sub-Saharan grasslands, called the Sahel. The Niger River flows through the country.

There are three main ethnic groups that live in Nigeria – the Hausa, Igbo, and Yaruba, plus many more minorities. There is much racism and vying for political power between the groups. The people are about half Muslim and half Christian, with a higher Muslim concentration in the north. Nigeria is a federal constitutional republic, with thirty-six states and the capital at Abuja. The government is modeled after the United States, but in practice is more like a banana republic of central America with severe instability because of corruption. There are problems with unlawful practices such as mistreatment of prisoners and harsh Sharia law in the north. There are also problems with gangs, drug lords, and pirates. Women are treated as a sub-class, with few property rights and lesser protection under the law. Polygamy is common in certain areas.

It is the most populous country in Africa and Lagos is one of the largest cities in the world. Its official language is English, though there are hundreds of tribal languages spoken as well. English was chosen as the language of education and government

Additional Layer

In Nigeria extended families live, work, and play together. They depend on a large family unit for support and help in times of need.

The extended family used to be the backbone of life in western nations as well, but the role of helping in times of need has been shifted and extended families are less important than they once were.

Where do people go if they need financial assistance in your country? Compare the two systems.

Photo shared on Wikimedia under CC license.

Additional Layer

English is the most common language in the world. It is today's language of business and culture, just as Latin was the common language of the middle ages. What made English the common language?

Additional Layer

As in other developing countries, the education of Nigeria's girls is seen as a major goal in eradicating poverty, disease, and generational war. You see, it's the girls who teach and train and feed and love the next generation of people. The problem is that, with limited resources, families will send their boys to school and keep their girls home since boys become the bread winners later on.

Think of specific ways the education of girls helps society.

How could the education of girls be encouraged in a country like Nigeria?

Photo shared on Wikipedia under CC license.

Fabulous Fact

The climate in northern Nigeria is very arid and hot. In the south it is still hot, but the ocean keeps it humid and wet.

The north is desert and grasslands, while the south is dense tropical rainforests.

since no native language is universal or near universal and the English lately governed Nigeria.

Anciently this is where the Nok people lived and it is thought to be the origin of the Bantu people who migrated throughout sub-Saharan Africa. Portuguese explorers found the area first among European nations and began to trade, especially in slaves. Most slaves brought to the new world came from this part of Africa.

In 1885, Britain claimed the area as a dependency. Slavery wasn't outlawed in Nigeria until 1936, though the British had been trying since 1807. On October 1, 1960 Nigeria became an independent nation. They have suffered through repeated military coups since then. In the 1970's oil was discovered and has been essential in the economic prosperity of the nation. In spite of this, the country has suffered from poverty and many millions have emigrated, over a million of them to the United States.

Lagos, Nigeria. Photo shared under CC license.

☺ ☺ ☺ **EXPLORATION: Map of Nigeria**
You can find a map of Nigeria at the end of this unit. Use a student atlas to complete the map.

Label these cities:
Lagos
Ibadan
Ogbomosho
Kano
Abuja

Color the map according to population. Use three colors in the same color family or different shades of the same color. The darkest should be the most populated regions and the lightest the least populated.

☺ ☻ EXPLORATION: Nigeria's Flag

Nigeria's flag has a white central stripe flanked by two green stripes. The white stands for peace and unity and the green stands for agriculture and natural resources. Make a flag using green paints on white paper.

☺ ☻ ☻ EXPLORATION: The Talking Drum

The talking drum is a traditional musical instrument from west Africa, including Nigeria. It is still used today in popular music. It is held under the arm to play. The two ends are made of skins stretched tightly and held with cords. When the skins are tightened more the pitch of the drum changes. When drumming, players will squeeze the drum with their arm to tighten or loosen the bands and control the pitch as they strike the drum with a curved stick.

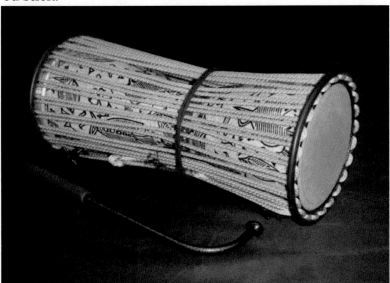

Photo by ɔ and shared under CC license on Wikimedia.

On the Web

Here is the complete text of a book of Nigerian Folk tales.

http://www.sacred-texts.com/afr/fssn/

Read a few tales and do a book project about one of them.

- Make a diorama box

- Re-tell the stories with puppets

- Paint a scene from the stories

- Make masks of the characters

Fabulous Facts

Nigeria has a population of about 120 million people, the eighth most populous country on earth.

It has a 50% literacy rate and is climbing steeply as a government-funded, mandatory education system catches up to the next generation.

It is about two and a half times the size of California in terms of land area.

Fabulous Fact

Oil is extremely important to the economy of Nigeria. They are a member of OPEC and about 40% of their income as a nation comes from oil.

They also have a growing technological and telecommunications section, manufacturing, and agriculture.

Famous Folks

Chinua Achebe is a Nigerian author and university professor who wrote the world famous novel *Things Fall Apart.*

Photo by Stuart C. Shapiro and shared under CC license.

Additional Layer

Racism is a big problem in Nigeria. Here is an article that hypothesizes that the manipulation by the colonial British made the problem much worse. See what you think.

http://www12.georgetown.edu/students/organizations/nscs/capitalscholar/lancia2.html

It is called a talking drum because it mimics the language of the people. If you are from the same village as the drummer you could literally understand the words the drum is speaking. West African languages are tonal. This means that when the pitch of a sound is varied, the meaning of the word is different. No matter how we say the word cat in English it is always a small furry animal with sharp teeth and claws. But in a tonal language the pitch or inflection of a word completely changes its meaning. Thus the drum can literally talk depending on the tone and pitch and rhythm and inflection.

Make a talking drum from two plastic plant pots, fabric and string.

1. Choose pots that are terra cotta or brown in color.
2. Glue the narrow ends of the pots together using hot glue and then use duct tape around the join.
3. Next, you need two circles of fabric, about an inch or larger in diameter than the wider end of the pot. Brown or tan colored fabric will be best.
4. Punch holes all around the edges of the fabric.
5. Place the fabric circles over each end of the drum and weave string in and out of the holes in the fabric, tying the fabric of each end to the other and stretching it tight.
6. Use a bent shaped kitchen utensil as your hitting stick.

Listen to juju music from Nigeria, a modern music that uses the traditional talking drum. Look for *King Sunny Ade-365 Is My Number* on You Tube.

☺ ☺ ☻ **EXPLORATION: Gourd Carving**
Gourd carving is a folk art practiced in Nigeria to make their everyday eating vessels more beautiful. Nowadays not many Nigerians eat from gourds, but they still display the carved gourds as beautiful pieces.

Carved gourd courtesy of the Brooklyn Museum.

You can carve a gourd. You need gourds from the supermarket or your garden and carving tools such as those used for carving pumpkins or used in pottery.

1. Cut the top off of your gourd and clean it out. (We recommend small gourds so the project doesn't become overwhelming.)
2. Draw the design you want on your gourd with a pen.
3. Carve the design out using the carving tools.
4. Now paint the gourd, making the carved areas dark, while the raised areas are brightly colored or light and uniform.

The designs used are geometric or a combination of geometric with flowers, plants, and animals.

☺ ☻ ☻ EXPLORATION: Jollof Rice

Jollof rice is a red rice from West Africa. The red color comes from the tomato mixture it is cooked in. Here's the recipe:

2 cups white rice	1 tsp. salt
8 oz. tomato sauce	1/4 tsp. cayenne pepper
3 oz. tomato paste	2 cubes chicken bouillon
1 diced onion	1 clove garlic, minced
water	

1. Boil 3 cups of water in a pot over medium high heat.
2. Once boiling, add the rice and let it cook for 15 minutes.
3. Once the rice is cooked, add the tomato sauce, tomato paste, onion, garlic, and seasonings. Continue to let it cook until the rice is tender, the sauces are incorporated, and the liquid has evaporated.
4. You can pair this rice with vegetables like red peppers or any kind of meat.

☺ ☻ ☻ EXPEDITION: Lagos

It's not likely you're planning a trip to Nigeria soon, but using You Tube you can peek into what it's like there. Try searching for these videos:

Nigeria's worst place to live

Additional Layer

Football (soccer to us) is the national sport and the most famous pastime in Nigeria. It can be seen played in every small village and every big city of the country. Wherever kids are gathered, there will likely be a game going. Small children there learn to create makeshift balls from banana leaves or rags so they can get a game going even when a ball isn't available. It's common to see a game going on in the street, stopping when necessary to let traffic go by.

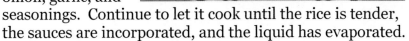

Tape Nigeria facts to a soccer ball and have the kids sit in a circle rolling the ball to one another. As each child gets the ball they get to take off and read one fact. Or for review, have questions in place of the facts.

Fabulous Facts

At Christmastime the cities of Nigeria empty as people return to their ancestral villages, where their family members still live. Those who have "made it" in the city give money and gifts to their rural relatives.

Additional Layer

Nigeria is divided by religion, with a heavily Muslim population in the north and a heavily Christian population in the south. The differences have caused political problems too, as the nine states in the north have adopted Sharia law. There are still issues about whether it is legal under the Nigerian constitution.

The Nigerian National Mosque in Abuja. Photo by Shiraz Chakera , CC license.

Read this article:

http://www.washingtonp ost.com/wp-dyn/content/article/200 9/08/11/AR2009081103 257.html

Writer's Workshop

Write a travelogue of what you imagine it would be like to go on an African safari.

About Abuja Nigeria
Music from Nigeria
Cross River Gorilla
Amazing creatures in South Africa (SA Tourism, Nigeria)

☺ ☺ ☻ EXPLORATION: Adire Cloth

Adire cloth is a Yoruba handcraft from the south western part of the country. The cloth is always done with indigo (dark blue) dye in a batik or tie dye sort of pattern. You can look up examples of Adire online.

Watch this short video to see three techniques used in making Adire: http://youtu.be/nELccoG-PcA

Now get some dark blue synthetic dye and white fabric from the store and create some of your own.

1. Start with a square of white cloth. Divide the square into nine even parts.
2. Use fabric starch to paint on your design. Let it dry thoroughly for several days before you dye it. If you like you can use stencils.
3. Dye your fabric in the dark blue dye according to the package directions. Make sure the dye is cool before dying or you will wreck your design.
4. Wash and dry your fabric.

☺ ☺ EXPLORATION: Nature in Nigeria

Nigeria is a very diverse natural area, including areas of rainforest, jungles, savannahs, and mountain lands. Gorillas live deep in the jungles. Giraffes, elephants, lions, antelopes, cheetahs, and zebras dot the savannahs. Unfortunately, many species of animals here are dying out because of hunting and habitat destruction.

Use construction paper, scissors, markers, and glue to create animal masks.

☺ ☺ ☻ **EXPLORATION: Say It 3 Ways**

In Nigeria people commonly speak three different languages – Yoruba, Ibu, and Hausa. Try to say these simple phrases in each language.

Thank you

Yoruba	E se
Ibu	Imela
Hausa	N'a gode

Welcome

Yoruba	E kaabo
Ibu	Nno
Hausa	Sanu de

Goodbye

Yoruba	O dabo
Ibu	kachifo
Hausa	S'aryuma

☺ ☻ **EXPLORATION: Mimic Me**

In Nigeria they play a clapping mimic game. You sit across from your partner and clap out a rhythm. You can include regular claps, kneeslaps, snaps, etc. Your partner tries to mimic the pattern. You keep making them harder and longer until they can't mimic it anymore.

Additional Layer

Nigeria has a bad case of "Brian Drain," a condition where many of the country's most highly educated in medicine, technology, and other fields leave to work in places like Britain and the United States, leaving their own country without the needed people.

Fabulous Fact

In south-west Nigeria and Benin a holiday called Gelede is celebrated annually with drumming, carefully choreographed dancing, and singing.

Photo by Grete Howard and shared under CC license.

The ceremony is performed by men and honors women as wise elders of the community.

Additional Layer

Nigeria is officially a federated constitutional republic. It has thirty-six states and a capital territory, Abuja.

The nation has had a great deal of unrest and alternated between military and elected governments as the people struggle to gain education, economic stability, and throw off colonial attitudes.

The elections are riddled with abuse and corruption, military forces often seize power through coups, and ethnic violence is frequent and widespread.

But there is hope as more and more Nigerians become educated and economic progress is made with the help of oil money and freer markets.

Read this article about the 2007 Nigerian elections. http://www.guardian.co.uk/world/2007/apr/24/chrismcgreal.international.al

How important are free and fair elections in a republic? What are the costs of corruption?

Nigerian Palm Wine Music

http://youtu.be/qB7deqrpb40

☺ ☻ EXPLORATION: Nigerian Elections

Nigeria votes for a president with a straight popular vote. The candidate with the most votes wins, but the winner must also get at least 25% of the vote in 2/3 of the states. Unfortunately fraud, violence, and general corruption have spoiled the confidence in

Woman voting during the 1999 election.

leadership. In 1999, the first civilian election in decades took place with Olusegun Obasanjo winning. Read this interview with Obasanjo following the election: http://www.pbs.org/newshour/bb/africa/july-dec99/nigeria_10-29.html

The Carter Center, founded by former United States President Jimmy Carter, observed and made a critical analysis of the election process of 1999. Read what they had to say.

http://www.cartercenter.org/news/documents/doc891.html

Do you think the 1999 election was fair? Why or why not?

Do you think "international observers" should interfere or comment on the political process in a nation?

Should international organizations interfere with elections they deem "unfair"? Why or why not? How would you like it if they interfered in your country's elections?

What is necessary for free and fair elections? Can those necessary elements be imposed by foreign nations? Should they be? Under what circumstances?

Look up the most recent Nigerian election. Have they improved?

SCIENCE: SKELETAL SYSTEM

Humans and many kinds of animals have skeletons to give form to their bodies. Animals with a backbone are called vertebrates and have an endoskeleton, which means the skeleton is inside the body. The adult human skeleton has 206 bones. Bones are made of living cells. The outer cells excrete minerals that harden and make bones stiff and strong. When babies first form inside their mothers their bones are made of cartilage. The bones harden slowly over time until you are about 25 years old, when they're as good as they'll ever get. That's one reason why you need good nutrition when you are young and growing. Inside the larger bones is a softer substance called marrow. The marrow makes red blood cells and stores fat.

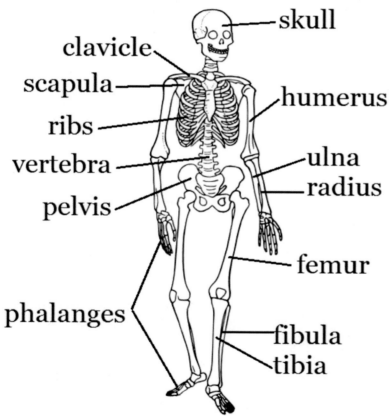

Bones are essential in movement. They are jointed, which means separate bones meet and have the ability to move. There are three types of joints: ball and socket, hinge, and fixed. We'll do some projects that will demonstrate how these different joints work.

☺ ☻ **EXPLORATION: My Amazing Body**
Make a picture of your insides. This project can be started now and continued over the next several units.

Memorization Station

Memorize the bones of the skeletal system. Older kids can manage more of them than younger kids.

Additional Layer

Learn more about the internal anatomy of bone.

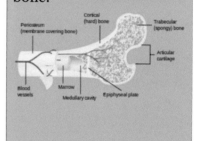

Famous Folks

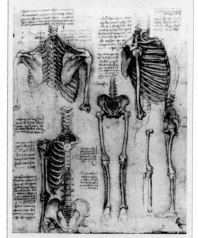

Leonardo Da Vinci dissected human bodies and studied the internal anatomy of humans more than five hundred years ago.

Fabulous Fact

Babies are born with 270 bones, but many of these fuse together as the child grows so that as adults humans have only 206 bones.

On The Web

Watch this video:

http://youtu.be/8d-RBe8JBVs

For a great overview of the skeleton in a 7 min video.

Additional Layer

Learn about how the skeletons of other animals function in the way that that animal needs.

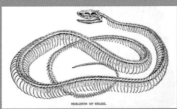

What is special about a snake skeleton?

Or a rabbit skeleton?

1. Get large sheets of butcher paper and trace your body onto the paper with the help of a friend.
2. Draw the major bones of your skeleton inside the picture of your body.

Later you can add your digestive system, cardiovascular system and so on.

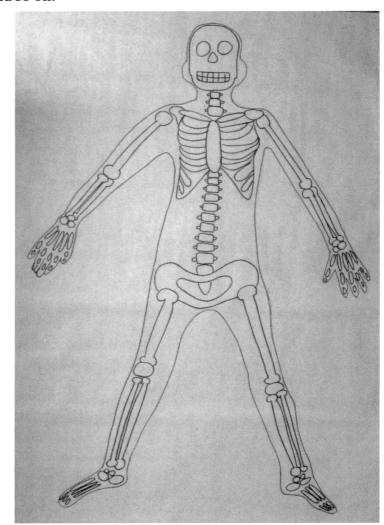

☺ ☻ EXPLORATION: No Bones

What do you think your body would look like without any bones? Have each kid draw a picture of themselves without any bones. You may want to show the movie clip from Harry Potter and the Chamber of Secrets when Professor Lockhart dissolves the bones in Harry's arm and it becomes a floppy stub.

After each person explains their picture ask whether or not we would be able to move without bones. Our muscles wouldn't have anything to attach to; our bodies aren't equipped for movement without our musculoskeletal systems.

☺ ☻ ☻ **EXPLORATION: Three Uses of Bones**

Bones do three things for us:
1. They provide structure to hold up our bodies.
2. They protect us. (Like our skull protects our brain and our rib cage protects our heart and lungs.)
3. They, together with muscles, help us to move. (This is especially true of the bones in our arms and legs.)

Look at a picture of a skeleton and find examples of bones that fulfill each of these uses. Then copy down the three uses of bones and put it in your science notebook.

☺ ☻ **EXPERIMENT: Popping Joints**

Joints pop because pressure inside the fluid of your joints dissolves gas bubbles. Pop a knuckle or another joint and see how long it takes for the liquid to redissolve the gas so you can pop the same joint again.

☺ ☻ **EXPERIMENT: What Makes Bones Hard?**

1. Pour 1 cup of vinegar into a clear container, like a liquid measuring cup or drinking glass.
2. Place a chicken thigh bone into the vinegar.
3. Cover the container (just because of the smell factor)
4. Let it sit for a week, checking everyday to see how the bone is doing.

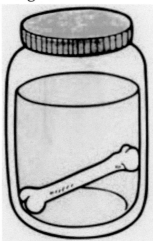
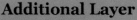

The bone will get all soft and rubbery starting with the ends first. The vinegar dissolves the calcium and other minerals. Calcium is the main mineral that makes bones hard. You can see bubbles forming on the bone; this is the reaction taking place.

☺ ☻ ☻ **EXPLORATION: What's Inside A Bone?**

Soup bones are available at most grocery stores or butcher shops. If you can't find a pre-packaged one, ask the butcher to slice a soup bone into 1"-2" long pieces to reveal the inner structure of the bone. You'll be able to see the layers of bone and the marrow. The outside layer is hard. Many bones are spongy inside and have lots of air holes. Marrow is the jelly-like center of the bone, and is the place where our blood is made.

Draw and label a diagram showing what you find in the soup bone.

Fabulous Fact

Human Skeletons show dimorphism, which means that males and females have different features. Males have longer leg and arm bones, narrower pelvises, thicker, heavier bones, and wider rib cages than females.

Additional Layer

Some people say we are taller in the morning when we wake up then we are in the evening when we go to bed. Being upright during the day makes vertebrae, hip bones, and knee bones settle closer together. At night, when we lie down, they stretch and lengthen again. Try it out for yourself. Have someone measure you in the morning and at night for a few days and compare.

Additional Layer

You can dissolve a chicken egg shell, just like you dissolved the minerals in the bone with vinegar. A chicken's egg is mostly hard because of the calcium.

Additional Layer

Calcium regulation

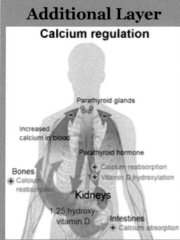

The body keeps calcium balanced at exact levels in order to keep muscle contractions, thyroid functions, cell functions, and other body systems working. If you are not ingesting enough calcium, your body resorts to using the calcium from your bones. Poor nutrition in young people can result in stunted or abnormal growth, and in adults it can lead to bone disease, fractures, and osteoporosis.

Additional Layer

Georgia O'Keefe often painted bleached skulls and bones of the desert. Look up some of her paintings and try one of your own.

Fabulous Fact

Humans and giraffes have the same number of neck bones.

☺ ☺ ☻ EXPLORATION: How Much Do Bones Weigh?

If bones were solid they would be much heavier than they are. Our bones weigh about 1/7 of our body weight. Have each student figure out the weight of their bones.

☺ ☺ ☻ EXPLORATION: Calci-YUM

Our bones need calcium so they can be strong. Make a list of foods we eat that have calcium in them. For a few days, record the foods you eat and how much calcium you get from those servings.

Toddlers need about 500 mg of calcium daily. Kids need about 800 mg. Teens need 1300 mg. Adults 19-50 need about 1000 mg. Adults over 50 need about 1200 mg.

☺ ☻ EXPERIMENT: Model Hinge Joint

Our joints provide flexible connections between our bones. Without joints we would be stiff. We couldn't walk up stairs, drive a car, or wave hello. Hinge joints work just like a door hinge, allowing you to move back and forth, much like a door moves back and forth.

To make a model hinge joint, just attach two craft sticks together with a rubber band, in an X pattern, so the joint can move with resistance from the rubber band. The craft sticks are like the bones and the rubber bands are like the ligaments, that control and limit motion.

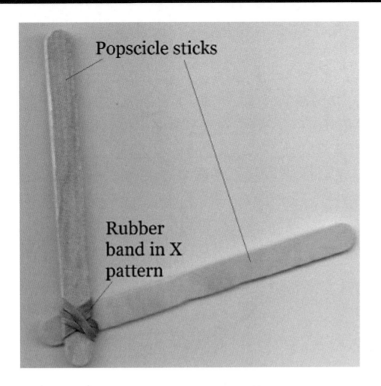

Popscicle sticks

Rubber band in X pattern

Where are these joints found? Knees, elbows, toes . . .

☺ ☻ EXPLORATION: Diagram of the Knee

Your knee is a hinge joint. The ligaments and cartilage around the bones helps to limit the movement of the knee and to cushion and protect it. A knee gets a lot of hard usage, especially when you run and jump, so it needs to be built well. Use the diagram of the knee from the end of this unit. This is a view of the knee from the front, when the knee is bent; as though you are looking straight at someone's knee, sitting in a chair. The name of the part is listed, a coloring description, and description of the part and how it works. The colors are obviously not realistic, they just help you to visualize the different parts.

A numbered description of each part and how it works:

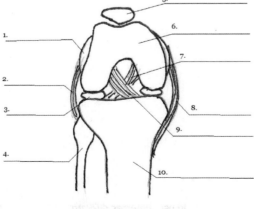

1. Femur. Color yellow. This is the thigh bone. In this view you are looking at the end of the bone, near the knee.
2. Collateral ligament. Color pink. Attaches the femur to the fibula. Ligaments stabilize the knee.

Writer's Workshop
Write an informational pamphlet about the importance of nutrition for bone health. Do some research and include accurate facts and statistics.

Additional Layer

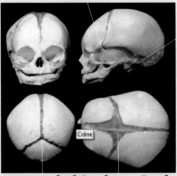

Human babies have "soft spots" or fontanelles on their heads. These are places where instead of bone, there is cartilage. These soft spots are necessary for the baby to be born so that his or her skull can flex as it passes through the birth canal.

After the baby is born the soft spots remain until the baby is nearly a year old, so you have to be especially careful with their heads.

Additional Layer

Learn the first aid for a broken bone. What would you do if you were far from a hospital?

Poor Harrison broke his arm on the trampoline.

On the Web

Crayola.com has a printable simple human skeleton diagram for you to fill out the names of main bones in the body. http://www.crayola.com /free-coloring- pages/human- skeleton.aspx

Exploration

Roughly cut out the skeleton pieces in the worksheet at the end of this unit and glue or tape them together.

Garrett is pretending to be sad because "this guy is dead!"

This one keeps it from moving side to side.

3. Meniscus. Color blue. Pads of cartilage that cushion the bones and act as shock absorbers.
4. Fibula. Color yellow. The smaller bone in the lower leg.
5. Patella. Color yellow. Also called your kneecap, it is a bone that protects the front of your knee joint from damage.
6. Articular cartilage. Color blue. Covers the underside of the femur, there is also articular cartilage covering the end of the tibia, fibula and patella. It cushions and protects the joint.
7. Posterior cruciate ligament (PCL). Color pink. Posterior means backside in anatomy so this ligament is behind the other. It limits the backward motion of the knee joint.
8. Collateral ligament. Color pink. Limits sideways motion of the knee.
9. Anterior Cruciate Ligament (ACL). Color pink. Anterior means in front. This ligament limits forward motion of the tibia and keeps the knee joint from rotating. This one is often injured by people.
10. Tibia. Color yellow. This is the larger bone in the lower leg.

☺ ☻ **EXPERIMENT: Model Ball and Socket Joint**
1. Roll a ball of clay or play dough to fit inside a plastic Easter egg shell.
2. Stick a craft stick (or any stick) down inside the clay.
3. Roll the clay ball around inside the Easter egg shell.

This model is like two bones that come together in a ball and socket joint. They can roll around in all directions. Which joints move like this? Your hip and shoulder are two. But these joints also have ligaments to restrict movement and control the joint.

☺ ☻ EXPERIMENT: Model Vertebra

You need wood blocks, a kitchen sponge, and two rubber bands.

1. Get two similar sized blocks of wood, like kids building blocks.
2. Cut a kitchen sponge to fit between the blocks of wood. You want three or four layers of sponge.
3. Use two rubber bands to hold all three layers together: wood, sponge, wood.

You can move the joint by pressing on one side or the other and the joint can expand and contract a little. This is like a vertebra joint. Each individual vertebra can move just a little, but together the whole spine can bend quite a ways. The rubber bands are like the ligaments, controlling and restricting the motion. The sponge is like the cartilage, cushioning the joint. The wood blocks are like the bones.

☺ ☻ ☻ EXPERIMENT: Model Cranial Joint

Your skull isn't just one big bone, it is actually several bones fused together. The joints between the bones are like puzzle pieces that lock together and prevent movement.

To demonstrate this, find a puzzle and examine how the pieces lock together. What if the sides were straight? Would the puzzle stay together? Try making a straight sided puzzle from cardboard and compare it with a jigsaw puzzle.

Additional Layer

The carpal tunnel is a narrow passage through the bone and connective tissue in the wrist, which a nerve passes through to the hand. In some people the nerves become irritated and cause great pain, even permanent crippling if untreated. This is called carpal tunnel syndrome.

Memorization Station

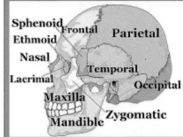

Memorize the bones of the skull.

All the bones in the skull are fused together except for the mandible.

On The Web

Visit http://www.innerbody.com/anatomy/skeletal-male

to see the human skeleton in detail. Choose the male or female skeleton and then click on individual bones to get descriptions of each one.

Fabulous Fact

Bones are alive, growing, repairing, producing parts of our body, not just dead structural pieces.

Additional Layer

Isaac Newton was knighted and allowed to adopt a coat of arms.

He chose the ancient one of the baronet Newton family to which he was related: two crossed shin bones on a black field.

Additional Layer

Skeletons and bones are used as imagery to represent death or danger.

This skull and cross bones is often used as a warning of poison.

EXPLORATION: Simon Says Skeleton Style

Help learn the bones of the body by playing Simon Says. If you preface your instructions by saying "Simon says . . ." the players must do it, but if you leave that off they have to ignore your instructions. If they don't follow the instructions precisely, they are out. During this unit, use commands like, "Simon says touch your ulna." "Simon says wiggle your metatarsals." "Move your skull."

EXPLORATION: Pasta Skeleton

After reading a book about the skeleton with your little ones, give them some dishes of different shapes of pasta. Let them glue the pasta onto a sheet of construction paper to make a human skeleton. Have them look at a picture of a skeleton for reference.

THE ARTS: CANTERBURY TALES

You may think the Canterbury Tales are very old and very boring, but actually you'd only be half right. They are very old, but not boring in the least. The author, Geoffrey Chaucer, was not a pious modest model of propriety. He was rude and bawdy and irreverent . . . in fact, some of his stories are not at all appropriate for children. But they are also beautifully written poetry and a window into medieval English culture, besides their extraordinary entertainment value.

The tales are a series of stories within a story. To keep each other company and protect against bandits, a group of strangers is traveling together on a pilgrimage toward Canterbury Cathedral, a holy site on the south coast of England. To pass the time they tell one another stories along the way. Chaucer gives us a description of each storyteller, and the storyteller gives us their tale.

Depending upon the ages of your kids, refer to the book list at the beginning of the unit for suggestions on different versions of the Canterbury Tales. Read at least some of prologue and several of the tales during this unit.

☺ EXPLORATION: The Prologue
Memorize the Prologue to the Canterbury Tales in Middle English. You think we're joking? Not joking. You can do it, or at

---

On The Web
You can read all of the *Canterbury Tales* online here:

http://www.canterburyta les.org/

Fabulous Fact
Chaucer wrote this book at the end of the 1300's, a few decades after the Black Death and at a time when many people were questioning the teachings of the church.

Chaucer used the book to make fun of and draw caricatures of the church and its religious figures.

He also makes fun of other elements of English society.

You can take it seriously if you want to, but Chaucer would be disappointed.

Additional Layer
Just above in the Norman section we highlighted the murder of Thomas a Becket in the cathedral at Canterbury. It was the relics of Thomas a Becket that drew people to Canterbury in hopes of a miracle of healing or forgiveness in their lives. Chaucer is making fun of this very activity as well.

Writer's Workshop

JK Rowling based her "The Three Brothers" Tale from Beedle the Bard on the Pardoner's Tale.

http://youtu.be/BR939 M48BG4

Write your own version of a fairy tale based on one of Chaucer's.

least your kids can. Below we've written the Middle English version and with the modern English facing. This gives your kids a familiarity with the language of medieval English, the precursor of our own language, and helps them feel the rhythm and rhyme of Chaucer's original version. We actually only included the first twelve lines.

"w" is pronounced "v."
"i" sounds like "ee."
"ght" has a guttural sound, like you're clearing your throat.
"ed" at the end of a word has both the letters pronounc-ed. So you say the name "Ed" at the end of those words.

Here is a video of a guy reading it in Middle English so you can get the pronunciation: http://youtu.be/QEoMtENfOMU

1. Whan that aprill with his shoures soote	When April with his showers sweet with fruit
2: The droghte of march hath perced to the roote,	The drought of March has pierced unto the root
3: And bathed every veyne in swich licour	And bathed each vein with liquor that has power
4: Of which vertu engendred is the flour;	To generate therein and sire the flower;
5: Whan zephirus eek with his sweete breeth	When Zephyr also has, with his sweet breath,
6: Inspired hath in every holt and heeth	Quickened again, in every holt and heath,
7: Tendre croppes, and the yonge sonne	The tender shoots and buds, and the young sun
8: Hath in the ram his halve cours yronne,	Into the Ram one half his course has run,
9: And smale foweles maken melodye,	And many little birds make melody
10: That slepen al the nyght with open ye	That sleep through all the night with open eye
11: (so priketh hem nature in hir corages);	(So Nature pricks them on to ramp and rage)-
12: Thanne longen folk to goon on pilgrimages . . .	Then do folk long to go on pilgrimage . . .

Fabulous Fact

A Pardoner was a secular (not ordained) church official who sold indulgences, documents that would buy away sins, but Pardoners were often corrupt.

On The Web

Watch the Pardoner's Tale in cartoon (has a bloody, gory scene):

http://youtu.be/jPkhuvI 3Y8Y

Or watch this version:

http://youtu.be/h19FAS nB1vo

It just means that in the spring people go on pilgrimages.

After you get this memorized, definitely show off for the grandparents.

☻ ☻ EXPLORATION: Hero Couplet

The Canterbury Tales were written in poetry with rhyming couplets. A couplet is a set of two lines that rhyme with each other. Write a short heroic poem describing a famous person or someone you know, like your dad. Make sure you follow the couplet rhyme scheme.

☻ ☻ ☻ EXPLORATION: Frame Tale

A frame tale is just a story within a story. Generally, as in the Canterbury Tales, a frame tale takes a group of people who have gathered and are swapping stories. To emphasize this idea, begin with a shared writing experience. On a large sheet of paper (like butcher paper) begin a story, "Once upon a time . . ." Have each kid add a line or two with you as the scribe. Direct them ahead of time that their framework should include people getting together to swap stories in some format, on a vacation, around a campfire, over lunch at a restaurant, on a fishing trip, or on a walk. Encourage them to introduce the various players in the story as part of your shared writing paragraph. When the paragraph is complete, have each of them choose one character to write a story for. When you're done, put the introduction and all the stories together into one book. You've just made your own frame tale.

☺ ☻ EXPLORATION: Character Maps

Choose any of the characters within the prologue. Write his name in the middle of a sheet of paper or on a poster. Draw five boxes around the name with lines leading back to the name. At the top of each box write one of these words:

- Feelings
- Words
- Personality
- Appearance
- Motivations

Now search through the text and write descriptions of each. Use quotes from the text whenever possible. You may need to do a little historical research to put things into context if you aren't certain of the social position or professional details about a character.

The Miller from Canterbury Tales

☺ ☻ EXPLORATION: Cross Section of Society

The Canterbury Tales is a valuable piece of literature partly because it is so unique for its time. Most of the literature coming from this time period was written in the more proper English of the day and focused on the upper class. The Canterbury Tales used the English of the people and talked about all classes of people – millers, knights, priests, scholars, plowmen, and more. It gave us a clearer look at medieval society than other writings of the time.

Compare the coverage of the pilgrims in the tales to the coverage of modern people on media outlets today. Are the people on the news, prime time television, and entertainment news shows very representative of us today? What about on reality television? Have a discussion about the effects of what is on television on society as a whole? Does it affect you personally?

Famous Folks

Geoffrey Chaucer is considered the greatest medieval English poet. He was an author, courtier, astronomer, alchemist, and philosopher. He was born in London and grew up middle class in a well-to-do merchant's family. At one point during the Hundred Years War Chaucer, in company with some nobles, was captured and held in prison by the French. He was ransomed by the king for 16 pounds.

Writer's Workshop

What would the modern counterparts go on "pilgrimage" for? A trip to Disneyland? A political rally? The new release of a popular movie? What kind of event could draw many different people together in a way that they would have to interact? Set the scene and write it in your Writer's Notebook.

Additional Layer
Ezra Winter painted a mural on the wall at the Library of Congress depicting the Canterbury Tales. Here is a section of the mural:

You can see the whole mural here: http://upload.wikimedia.org/wikipedia/commons/4/4a/Canterbury-west-Winter-Highsmith.jpeg

From Michelle
My favorite Canterbury Tales version for the whole family is The Canterbury Tales Special Edition For Children edited by A. Kent Hieatt and Constance Hieatt, illustrated by Gustaf Tenggren.

Teaching Tip
I hardly ever read a story straight through, at least not a meaningful tale like Chanticleer. I pause and explain vocabulary or concepts; I ask the kids what they think will happen next; I ask them if they can spot the mistake such and such a character has made, and so on. It probably annoys the children.

☺ ☻ EXPLORATION: If Chaucer Wrote Today
Chaucer's tale-teller characters were not named. They were called simply by their professions, and described in generalizations. His characters are "types." If he wrote about our society today he would probably use some archetypical characters as well. Describe each of these professionals using stereotypes as Chaucer would.

   Lawyer
   Farmer
   Politician
   Banker
   Actress
   Mother
   Teacher
   Librarian
   Computer Programmer

Now come up with a few of your own to describe.

☺ ☻ ☻ EXPLORATION: Your Own Pilgrim
Read the introductions of several of the pilgrims from the prologue of *The Canterbury Tales*. Create your own pilgrim as in the story. Make a sketch and write a paragraph or two introducing the pilgrim. You might even want to pattern it on yourself.

☺ ☻ ☻ EXPLORATION: Your Pilgrim's Tale
Now take your pilgrim a bit further. Write a tale told by him or her after reading several of the original pilgrims' tales.

☺ ☻ EXPLORATION: Chanticleer
There is one tale in particular that appeals to children, while at the same time providing enough material for a doctoral thesis. It is the Nun's Priest's Tale, called Chanticleer and the Fox.

Read the re-telling of the story, *Chanticleer and the Fox* by Barbara Cooney. It's a Caldecott medal winner so it's probably in your library.

Next, you can make puppets of the three main characters of the story: Chanticleer the rooster, Partlett the hen, and the fox. First color the pictures (I had the kids color while I read since it keeps them quieter), then cut the figures out in a rough outline, and glue them onto thin cardboard, like from food packaging. Tape a craft stick to the back side. Alternatively, you can make them into flannel board figures by gluing a strip of sandpaper to the back.

Have the kids re-tell the story using their figures. Get the puppets from http://www.layers-of-learning.com/canterbury-tales-for-kids/ or from the end of this unit.

☺ ☻ ☻ EXPLORATION: The Knight's Tale

The knight tells the first tale and his is about courtly love and dashing knights in armor behaving absolutely ridiculously, all because they merely spied a beautiful maiden from the tower window. Chaucer uses several different genres of storytelling as each of the pilgrims tells his or her tale, presumably using the sort of tale that character likes best. The knight's tale is a typical medieval romance: knights and fair maidens in love, knightly manners, a far distant past, lots of honor and courage, great deeds, all the characters larger than life, trial by combat, and an ending that makes all the characters happy (even the dead ones).

In the knight's tale, two cousins, closer than brothers, are taken from a battlefield badly wounded after being defeated by Theseus of Athens. The two brothers are locked up in a tower, never to be released for fear they might threaten Theseus' kingdom, but from the tower window they spy Theseus' sister-in-law, the unwed Emily. They both fall in love with her and quarrel over her, turning their lifelong love into hatred in a moment. Through twists of fate the two cousins are released and escape respectively, and they meet later in a wood to combat to the death over this girl they still have never even met. Theseus happens upon them and stops the fight, but arranges a courtly battle to see who will win Emily's hand. The gods take a hand in the situation and begin to

Additional Layer

In the Franklin's Tale, a happily married wife is wooed against her will by a young man while her husband is away on a dangerous voyage. Very certain of his failure, she promises that she will be the young man's lover if he can make all the rocks on the coast of Brittany disappear. The young man gets a sorcerer to help him for a fee. The sorcerer, using his scientific knowledge tells the young man the rocks will disappear on a certain day. Owing to an exceptionally high tide, the rocks do disappear and the young lady is left with a problem.

Read the tale to find out how it ends.

Fabulous Fact

The Miller's Tale is one of the most rude and bawdy. Chaucer tells this tale right after the oh-so-refined Knight's tale as an answer to it.

arrange the fate of these mortals. One cousin wins, but immediately has an accident and dies; the other cousin gets to marry the girl and they live happily ever after.

Chaucer sets his medieval knights in ancient Greece, complete with gods and goddesses – not at all where they "belong". At the end of this unit you'll find two paper knights and a lady. Color them, cut them out, and glue their paper stand in a circle to make them stand up. Then raid your toy box and make a setting for them. It should be somewhere or some time that is anachronistic (a setting where medieval knights would not normally be found). It could be outer space, the American Revolutionary War, the age of the dinosaurs or some other scene. Older kids can write their own version of the knights in their anachronistic setting.

☺ ☺ ☻ EXPLORATION: The Wife of Bath

The story of the wife of Bath provides a very interesting look at women of the middle ages. In the story, when an old woman comes to the rescue of a knight he must return her goodwill by marrying her. He is not at all happy to be wed to an ugly, old woman. But then she reveals that she is a fairy, and she gives him an option: she can become a beautiful, unfaithful wife or an ugly, faithful wife. He leaves the choice up to her, encouraging her to choose the way that will make them both happiest. The fairy is so happy to have this power over her husband that she chooses to give him all that he wants – a beautiful and faithful wife.

Discussion Questions:
- What does this tale say about womens' place in society?
- Was age valued?

- Can you draw parallels between this story and feudalism?
- If you could choose to be either virtuous or beautiful, which would you choose?

At the end of this unit you will find a printable circle window craft to color and assemble. Cut out the windows in the first circle and place it over the top of the second circle, securing the two together with a brad in the center.

On the Web

Search for more of the Canterbury Tales on You Tube. Please preview, like we said, they're not all appropriate.

Additional Layer

After reading one of the tales, don't forget to discuss it. Each of the tales has themes. Chaucer was very well educated and he was making important points about his society. Get a literature guide to help you.

Then have your kids cement the tale in their minds by retelling it, acting it out or making a Lego short film of it.

Coming up next . . .

Unit 2-8

Feudal System
Germany
Muscles, Skin, &
Cardiopulmonary
Gothic Art

My Ideas For This Unit:

Title: _____   Topic: _____

_____

_____

_____

_____

_____

_____

_____

_____

_____

_____

Title: _____   Topic: _____

_____

_____

_____

_____

_____

_____

_____

_____

_____

_____

_____

_____

Title: _____   Topic: _____

_____

_____

_____

_____

_____

_____

_____

_____

_____

_____

My Ideas For This Unit:

Title: _____   Topic: _____

_____

_____

_____

_____

_____

_____

_____

_____

_____

Title: _____   Topic: _____

_____

_____

_____

_____

_____

_____

_____

_____

_____

_____

Title: _____   Topic: _____

_____

_____

_____

_____

_____

_____

_____

_____

_____

Joan of Arc

Joan of Arc was a teenage girl from a little village called Domrémy in France. When she was a child France was losing the Hundred Years War against the English. The peasants suffered greatly as armies moved through and life was disrupted. Joan believed she was called of God to save France. She convinced some noblemen and then the king to let her lead the French army. When she did, the French had great success and defeated the English.

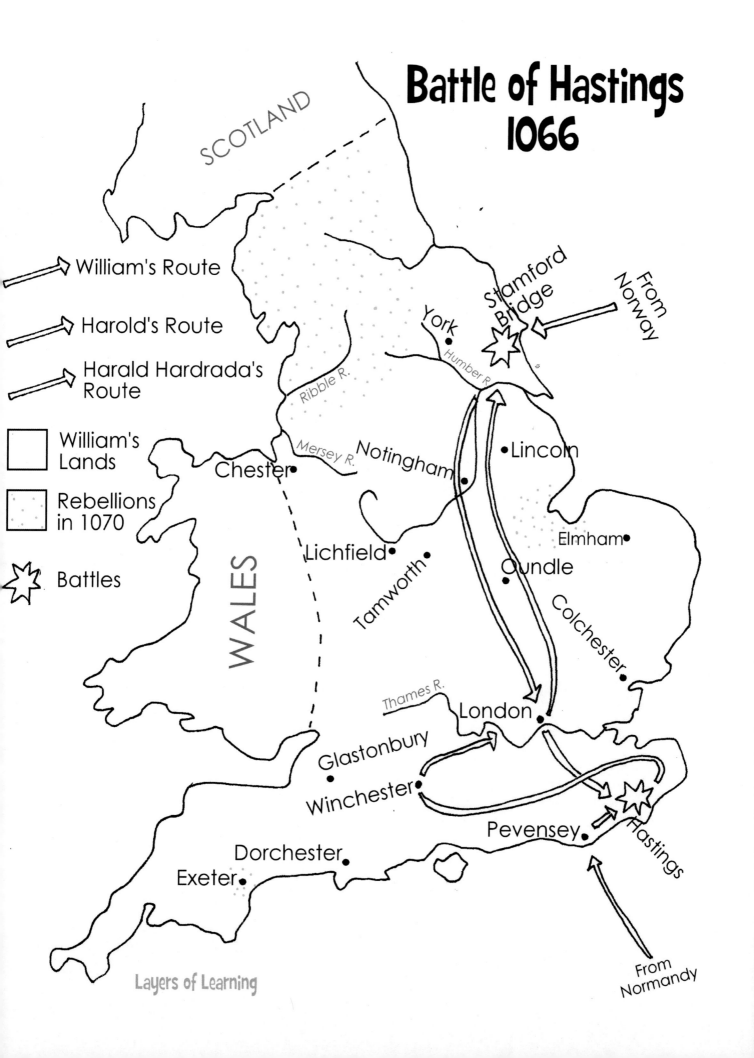

Battle of Hastings 1066

SCOTLAND

William's Route

Harold's Route

Harald Hardrada's Route

William's Lands

Rebellions in 1070

Battles

From Norway

Stamford Bridge

York

Humber R.

Ribble R.

Lincoln

Mersey R.

Notingham

Chester

Elmham

WALES

Lichfield

Oundle

Tamworth

Colchester

Thames R.

London

Glastonbury

Winchester

Pevensey

Hastings

Dorchester

Exeter

From Normandy

Layers of Learning

Normans: Unit 2-7

1042-1066 2-7

Reign of Edward the Confessor; Harold elected as successor

Sept 1066 2-7

Harald Hardrada of Norway is defeated at Stamford bridge

Oct 1066 2-7

Battle of Hastings; William becomes king

1069-1070 2-7

English in the north rebel and William ruthlessly puts down the rebellion

1135 2-7

War of succession between Matilda and Stephen, lasts 19 years; period known as "The Anarchy"

1170 2-7

Thomas a Becket is killed in Canterbury Cathedral

1275 2-7

Parliament begins to meet regularly in England

1284 2-7

England annexes Wales and crown prince is known as Prince of Wales from then on

1290 2-7

Edward expels Jews from England, culminating hundreds of years of persecution; in 1182 they had been driven from France

1296 2-7

Edward deposes Scot king, John Balliol

1297 2-7

Battle of Cambuskenneth, Scot, William Wallace, defeats English

1298 2-7

Battle of Falkirk, English defeat William Wallace

1305

William Wallace captured and executed

1306

Robert the Bruce defeats English again and is crowned king of Scots

1314

Battle of Bannockburn, Scots defeat English

1315-16

Famines in Europe mark a definite end to the prosperity of the High Middle Ages

1324-84

Life of religious reformer, John Wycliffe

1337

Start of 100 Years War

1340

Naval battle of Sluys, victory for England

1340

Geofrey Chaucer born

1340

English Parliament declares exclusive right to tax

1346

Battle of Crecy, English victory

1356

Battle of Poitiers, English Victory

1381

Peasants revolt and march on London

1415

Battle of Agincourt, English beat French

1429

Joan of Arc relieves the city of Orleans and helps Charles VII to be crowned king at Rheims

1430

Burgundians capture Joan of Arc and give her to the English; she is burned the next year

1453

100 Years War ends, English lose all continental territories

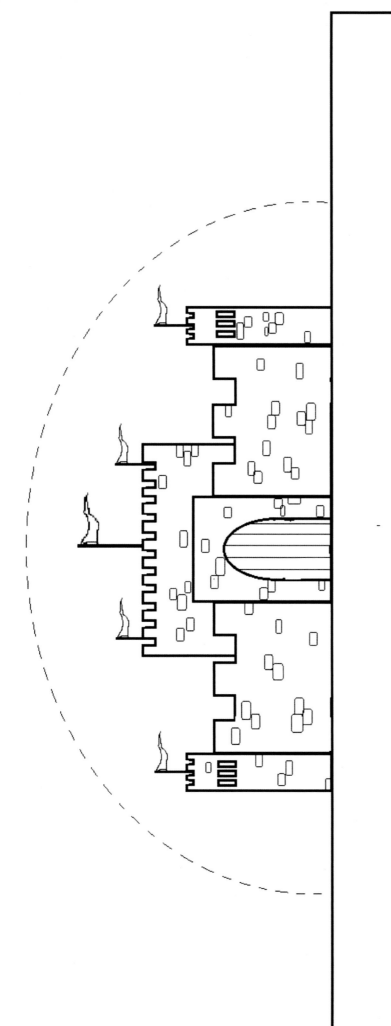

Protection of Life

People have no say in their government, government by tyranny

Protection of Property

Rule of Law: Laws are the same for everyone and are consistent

The law is upheld

Government is accountable to the people

Property is not respected

People have a say in government

Lawlessness and harm to persons or property are punished

Life is not considered sacred or valuable unless it is the life of the ruling class

Justice is vigilante, only enforced by the strong

Lawless behavior goes unpunished

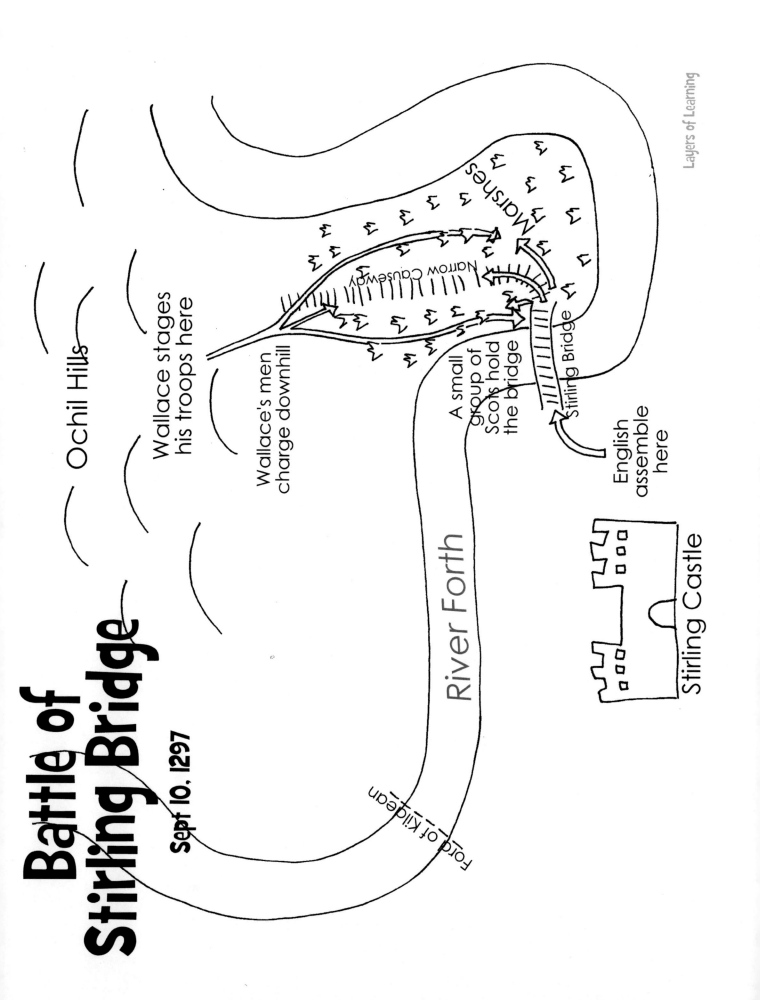

Battle of Stirling Bridge

Sept 10, 1297

Ochil Hills

Wallace stages his troops here

Wallace's men charge downhill

Narrow Causeway

Marshes

A small group of Scots hold the bridge

Stirling Bridge

English assemble here

River Forth

Ford of Kildean

Stirling Castle

Edward III's Coat of Arms

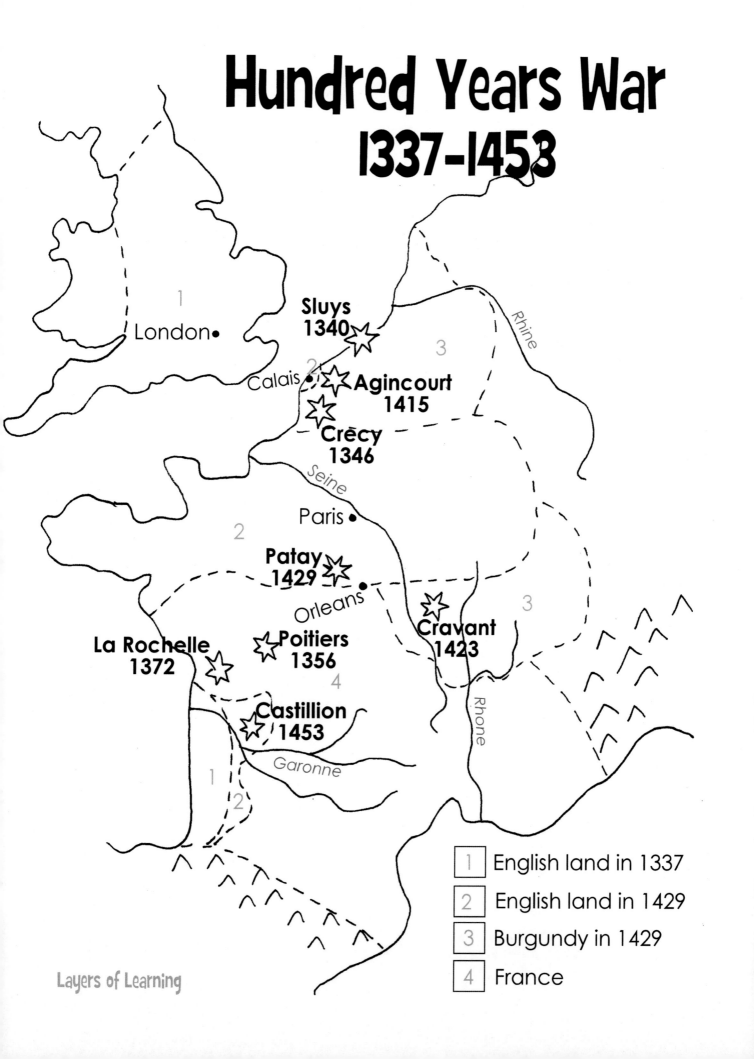

Hundred Years War
1337-1453

London•

Sluys
1340

Rhine

3

Calais•
Agincourt
1415

Crecy
1346

Seine

Paris•

2

Patay
1429

Orleans

Cravant
1423

3

La Rochelle
1372

Poitiers
1356

Rhone

4

Castillion
1453

Garonne

1

2

1	English land in 1337
2	English land in 1429
3	Burgundy in 1429
4	France

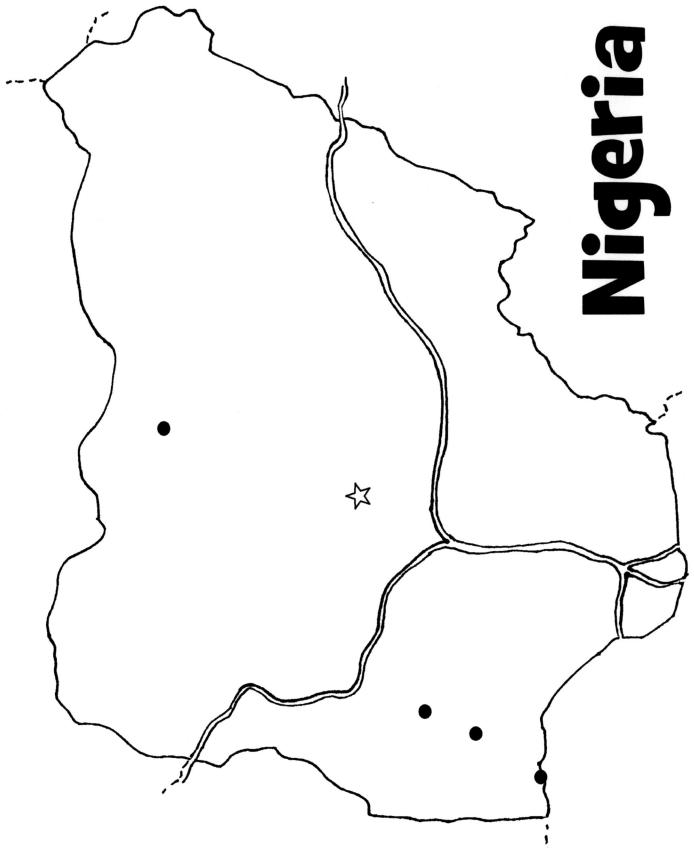

Nigeria

Knee Joint

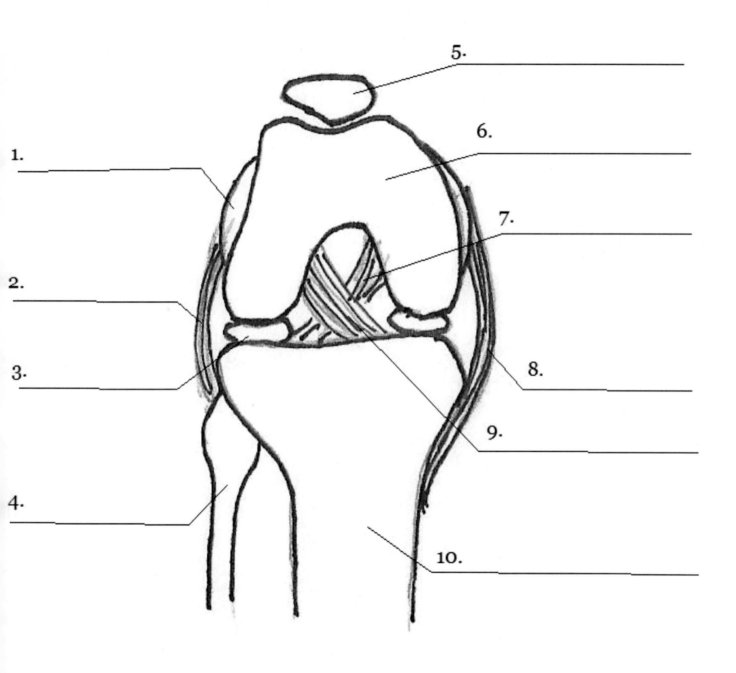

1.

2.

3.

4.

5.

6.

7.

8.

9.

10.

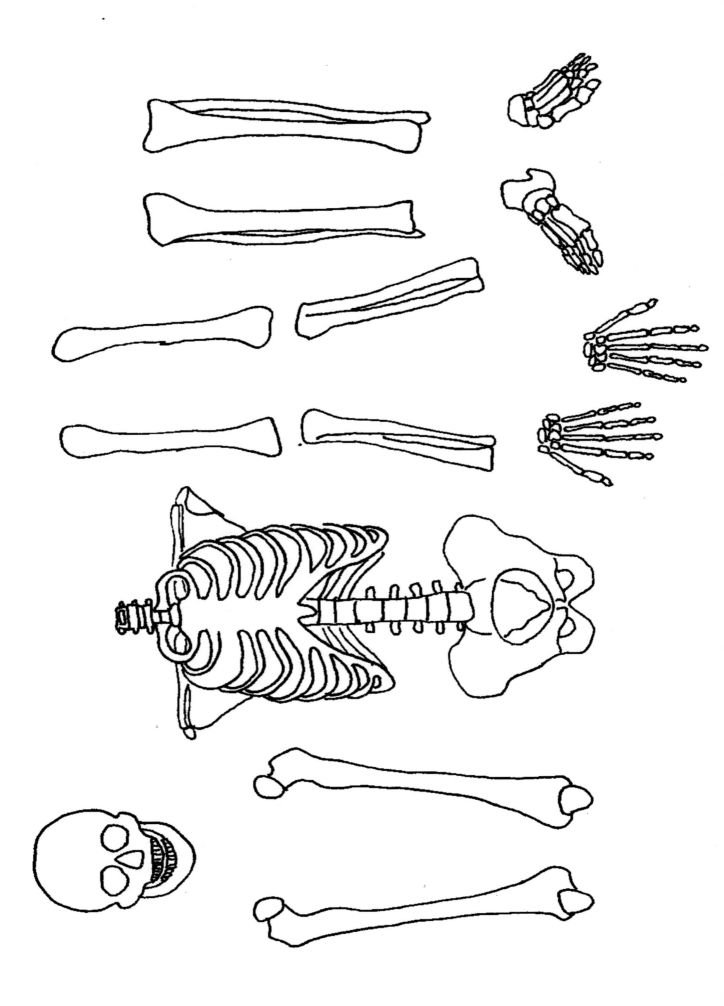

Chanticleer and the Fox

Read the re-telling of this story of Chaucer by Barbara Cooney. Color the animals, cut them out, glue them to thin cardboard and use them to re-tell the story in your own words.

Knight's Tale Figures

Print, color, cut out, and glue the stands together in a ring.

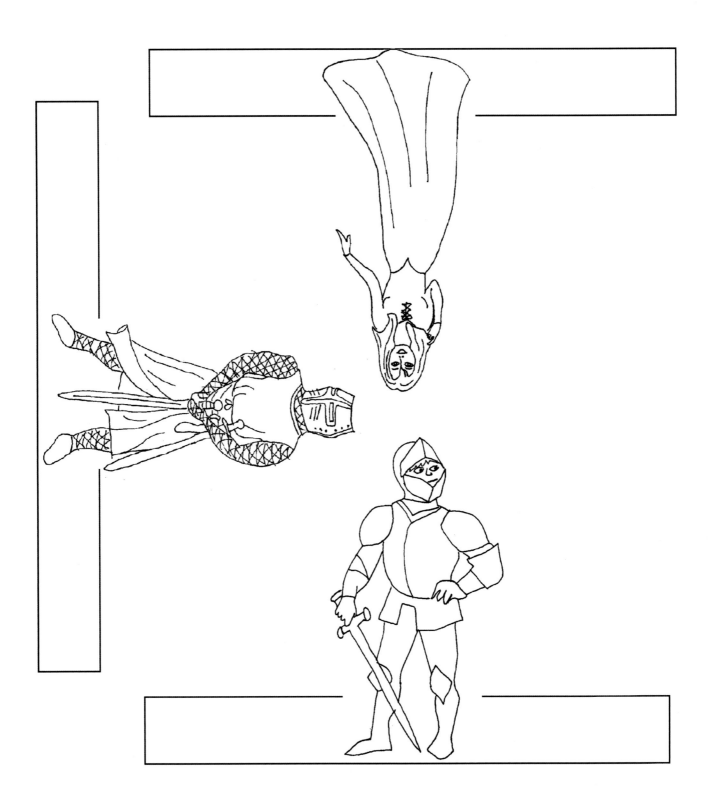

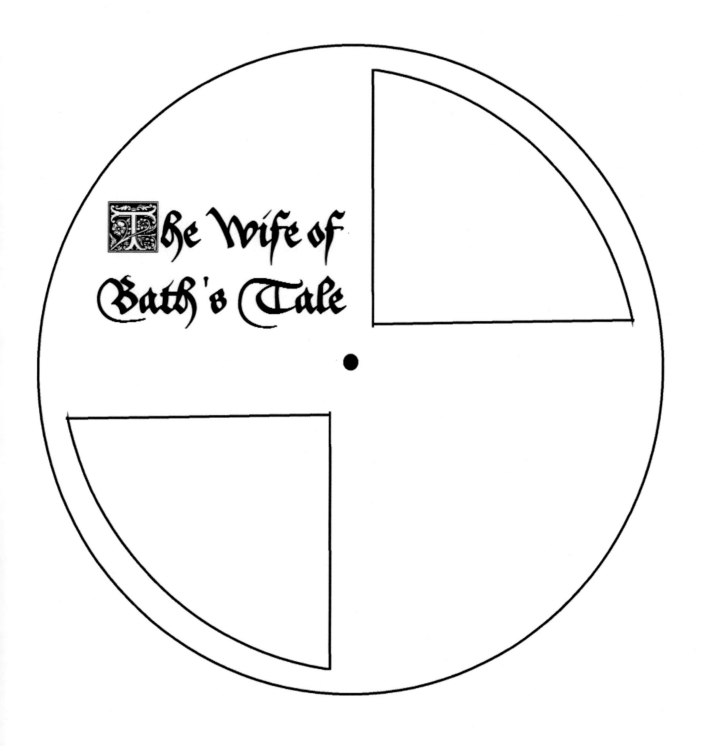

The Wife of Bath's Tale

ABOUT THE AUTHORS

Karen & Michelle . . .
Mothers, sisters, teachers, women who are passionate
about educating kids.
We are dedicated to lifelong learning.

Karen, a mother of four, who has homeschooled her kids for more than eight years with her husband, Bob, has a bachelor's degree in child development with an emphasis in education. She lives in Utah where she gardens, teaches piano, and plays an excruciating number of board games with her kids. Karen is our resident Arts expert and English guru {most necessary as Michelle regularly and carelessly mangles the English language and occasionally steps over the bounds of polite society}.

Michelle and her husband, Cameron, homeschooling now for over a decade, teach their six boys on their ten acres in beautiful Idaho country. Michelle earned a bachelor's in biology, making her the resident Science expert, though she is mocked by her friends for being the *Botanist with the Black Thumb of Death*. She also is the go-to for History and Government. She believes in staying up late, hot chocolate, and a no whining policy. We both pitch in on Geography, in case you were wondering, and are on a continual quest for knowledge.

Visit our constantly updated blog for tons of free ideas,
free printables, and more cool stuff for sale:
www.Layers-of-Learning.com

Made in the USA
Middletown, DE
04 April 2025

73769540R00038